TEN
DRINKS
THAT CHANGED
THE WORLD

For my parents
Cheers

TEN DRINKS THAT CHANGED THE WORLD

ACC
ART
BOOKS

CONTENTS

INTRODUCTION 9

BAIJIU 14

COGNAC 32

VODKA 52

SCOTCH & IRISH 72
WHISKIES

SHŌCHŪ 94

TEQUILA 114
&MEZCAL

BOURBON 134

RUM 154

GIN 176

ABSINTHE 194

INTRODUCTION

Welcome. It's a pleasure to have you here. We're about to spend some time together over a few drinks, but before we begin, I thought I'd tell you a little about why I wrote this book.

I think alcohol is similar to the element of fire. It was present long before we understood how to create it. Along with food and water, fire and alcohol were some of the earliest things that brought people together.

In my head, food and water are our necessities. We evolved from the seas and our need for water is still greater than our need for food. Although alcohol came about much later, like fire, it is a luxury; both occur naturally, but we had to learn to capture them. Their acquisition took imagination and continuing to use them meant sharing what we knew with others. Fire and alcohol required the human capacity to connect and to dream. It was while gathered around these necessities and luxuries that people passed ideas of what the world around them could become. To my mind, alcohol holds keys to understanding our ancestors and our lives today. It offers social, economic and political perspectives that can be as deep as the categories are broad. The destinies of both individuals and civilisations can be followed with alcohol – the stories of how we came to be the way we are.

The history of alcohol is less a history and more a story. Often records fail us or rumours bubble with the vigour of fermenting gloop. At times in the past, enough alcohol was sunk at get-togethers that people dropped dead from overconsumption, their tales perishing with them. Do we truly know how it all played out at the funerals of the Scots and Irish or at one of Prince Peter's pickled nights at the palace? These mysteries set alight the same imagination used to create spirits. They make us wonder at what isn't there just as much as we're in awe of what is.

What I wanted to give is a taste of the stories I think are captivating and a sense of how these drinks have shaped people's lives. That this is a relatively short book is a good thing. Hopefully it is a little more approachable for those who aren't ready to read a whole book on gin or bourbon or cognac. From my perspective the length has meant I simply couldn't cover the complete history of each spirit. I've had the luxury of searching centuries of stories and zooming in on those moments I thought had a great impact or were worth sharing. There are many fine books written on spirits. They go into far more detail about the history and cultural significance of these drinks than this one. This book then, I'd like to put forward as an introductory aperitif for the inquisitive. A flight of the flavours to be discovered should you acquire a taste for the lives of spirits.

No book on spirits written by a bartender would be complete without a few of their own recipes. The last drink in each chapter is one of my own (all six in chapters one and five). The first two drinks are what I believe to be fine ways to enjoy that spirit. It goes without saying there are innumerable recipes to be found, but I thought these would be excellent cocktails to start with.

Distillation came out of the quest of many early alchemists searching for the *quinta essentia*, the fifth element. The alchemists believed if they could find this element it would bring untold longevity, cure illness and turn metals into gold. Imagine their disappointment when what emerged from the still was a fiery liquid, which did no more to metal than water. In their attempts to strip away combined elements from one another, the alchemists discovered spirit. Over their lifetimes, spirits would preserve herbs and botanicals for medicines, be used by the military to combat disease and come to be used as currency. Perhaps the alchemists were closer than they first thought...

Seki Lynch

'Did I want one? Yes. I thought I would.
Pathetic. But what's the point of trying not
to drink? It's so bloody aimless isn't it?'

BAIJIU
白酒

It takes little stretch of the imagination to suppose the Chinese spirit, Baijiu, may be the oldest in existence. From merchants who carried their knowledge along the Silk Road, distillation technology married with sophisticated fermentation techniques in the imperial courts. The spirit produced has become one of unparalleled significance in Chinese culture. Yet baijiu has only recently begun to enjoy a reputation in world markets. Even then, most westerners have yet to hear of the spirit. Baijiu boasts a complex and unique fermentation process not used in any other drink on the planet. Once shunned as a farmers' respite, potent baijiu has risen to become revered by politicians and businessmen. Selling well over double that of its closest competitor, vodka, baijiu is by far the most consumed spirit in the world.

WHAT IS BAIJIU?

Pronounced 'bye-joe', baijiu is distilled from a single or blend of fermented grain. Sorghum, rice, wheat, barley and corn are common ingredients. In some instances, other members of the grass family are fermented to be distilled, such as millet and Job's tears (Chinese pearl barley). The raw material used depends on the desired flavour a producer wants to create. The three main categories of baijiu – light, strong and sauce (resembling soy sauce) – make up some 60-70% of

production. There are a further nine categories, however, each with their own unique production techniques. A great contributor to the flavour is the fermentation starter, qu. The blend of grains used in qu varies; it may contain wheat or barley, or even peas. The blend is ground then lightly moistened and moulded into a solid block. This ferments into a cocktail of microorganisms: many yeast strains, filamentous fungi, bacteria and actinomycetes. Once fermented and distilled, large earthenware pots are used to age the drink for months to years. Due to the great variety of different organisms acting on the raw materials, this process results in a rich complexity of flavours and aromas in the final product.

A UNIQUE CROP

Sorghum is a flowering member of the grass family, of which there are some 25 species. The prime species, Sorghum bicolor, is farmed everywhere from Africa and the Americas to south and central Asia. It's believed an ancestor of this common sorghum was first domesticated 6,000 years ago in the Egyptian Nabta Playa desert. The plant possesses many special attributes, which contributed to its popularity as a tradable crop. Sorghum is rare among other cereal grains as it can survive both arid, clayey soils and tropical climes. The plant is one of the most efficient grains at photosynthesis and water uptake. Some types of sorghum have short maturation cycles of around 75 days, allowing them to yield sustenance three times a year. With so many fine qualities, sorghum eventually found its way from Africa to China around 5,000 years ago along trade routes. Its use didn't become prevalent for alcohol fermentation until some 4,000 years later, but once it did sorghum became indispensable – especially in the production of the country's favourite spirit.

FLEDGLING FERMENTATION MYTHS

The Chinese have been drinking alcohol for around 8-9,000 years. It's uncertain whether Neolithic inhabitants fermented independently from their Mesopotamian counterparts. What is known is that these early brews were made of surplus rice, along with honey and fruits. 3,000-year-old ceramics from the ancient capital city of Anyang and the Changzikou burial site were discovered with booze preserved inside. These fascinating ferments revealed complex drinking habits. Made from a base of rice, the wines were blended with botanicals and tree resins. They allude to the integral role of alcohol in ancient Chinese societies. Cultural lives were steeped in drinking. It is from this that a rich tapestry of myths, legends and stories emerge.

The myths surrounding the discovery of fermentation in China actually do the lineage of brewers a disservice. Generally, they place fermentation far later than it actually occurred. The most common myth sets the son of the fifth ruler of the Xia Dynasty (2070-1600 BCE) as the half-cut hero. It is said Du Kang was faithfully watching over his flock of sheep and thought it best to store his rice in the hollow of a mulberry tree. After leaving the rice in the tree for too long, he returned to find the resulting mixture intoxicating. Another version tells of a young Du Kang squirrelling away food for an ailing uncle in another tree. Du Kang returns to find a substance, which most probably looked foul, but which

Du Kang still felt compelled to feed the sick man. Of course, after imbibing the tree rot, the uncle felt fantastic. For his dendrologous efforts, Du Kang was immortalised as the saint or god of wine, depending on where you are in China.

IMPERIAL COURTS & MEDICINE

The court of the Zhou Dynasty (1046-256 BCE) took their drinking very seriously. 110 people were in the employ of the court as alcohol officers. At first this seems inconsequent, until it becomes apparent that they had very different roles to the 340 service staff whose job it was to distribute drinks to guests. These were on top of the 170 specialists hired to attend to the preparation of six different types of alcohol. All in, the Zhou court employed 2,400 people in order to cater to the culinary and inebriant needs of their guests.

This seems excessive until ancient China's relationship with alcohol is understood. Calligraphy, also from the Zhou dynasty, reveals how alcohol was believed to have medicinal properties. The Mandarin character for alcohol from this period, *jiu*, lent itself to constructing the character for the word cure, *yi*. Two hundred years later in the Han Dynasty (206 BCE-220 CE), Wang Mang (45 BCE-23 CE) extolled alcohol and crystallised the attitude that booze was health-giving, stating that it was, 'the oldest of a hundred medicines.' China's intimate relationship with alcohol as a medicine would be honoured later with baijiu. Some baijius are still infused with everything from ginseng to snakes for remedial purposes.

For centuries, the Chinese have used fermentation not only to produce alcohol but to preserve food supplies. Through design, experimentation or luck, a new mode of fermentation developed. Thousands of years ago, before distillate poured from a still, the Chinese found a far more sophisticated way to ferment than simply using yeast.

QU - A SOPHISTICATED ORGANISM

Pronounced 'chew', qu is a block of chosen grains or rice, compacted and dried as a host for microorganisms. This includes many yeast strains, fungi and bacteria. The inspiration for qu probably came from mouldy grain. But the acknowledgment of what qu could do meant Chinese producers created a unique fermentation method. Qu breaks down starch into necessary sugars before initiating spontaneous fermentation. This makes fermentation more economical than when using just yeast. The economics are particularly prevalent with grains, which require malting to convert

starches to sugars. It is believed this complex block of living matter was first used during the Han Dynasty (206 BCE–220 CE). The qu not only provides a far more efficient and effective way of fermenting, it also contributes hugely to flavour.

Qu comes in an infinite array of different compositions. Most distillers make their own qu because of the unique flavours it gives. That said, despite the combination or quantity of ingredients, qu comes in two basic forms. The first is small qu, generally made of rice and/ or glutinous rice. Small qu is cooked and rolled into balls, then left in an ambient room to grow additional cultures. These rice balls are sometimes formed with herbs running through them, telling of a medicinal past. Small qu is prepared to make both baijiu and yellow wine. Big qu is usually made from sorghum, mixed with other grains such as wheat, barley or peas. Once ground and moistened, the materials are moulded into large blocks. These are left to rest for a month or two, collecting moulds and other wonders as they dry, before being used to make baijiu.

Even with the world's most advanced fermentation material, the Chinese were missing one key element to make distillate. When qu was coupled with the technology of distillation, it made a phenomenally unique spirit.

THE BIRTH OF DISTILLATION & PESKY POETS

The essential philosophy behind spirits is generally attributed to the Greeks. In *Meteorologica*, Aristotle (384-322 BCE) outlines a theory that all liquids are water and their nature is characterised by admixtures. The philosopher goes on to say that the compositions of liquids can be manipulated through condensation. He gives the example of sea water, which when evaporated contains less salt that before. Aristotle mentions evaporation and condensation experiments with seawater, but agonisingly fails to divulge his methods. He got it right did Aristotle, when he said that wine, condensed, would become water, but not wholly. The conclusion of the eloquently constructed argument meant, at least at the time of writing, that Aristotle didn't scrutinise what else wine might produce. Unfortunately, this meant Aristotle would never taste 'the water of life', a name that would follow distilled alcohols throughout their existence. This essence, the alchemists believed, was the spirit of the plant they'd distilled.

From here the intellectual dialogue between Greece, Egypt and the Middle East spurred progress towards distillation. In the 3rd century lived Maria Hebraea, an alchemist working in Hellenistic Alexandria, Egypt. Her scientific practice enjoyed a complementary co-existence with mastery of material craftsmanship, including glass and metallurgy. Though much of her work perished, future alchemists honoured her ideas, accrediting her with the creation of the alembic still. Maria's distillation didn't involve alcohol, but the principal seed took root and eventually the technique travelled. The Arabs translated many Egyptian texts. Reaching the bosom of the Islamic Enlightenment, distillation knowledge was refined and put to use with alcohol.

The strict Muslim, Jabir Ibn Hayyan, who died in 815 CE, is often cited as the first to comprise a written record of distilling spirit from wine. The word alcohol actually comes from the Arabic 'al-kuhl'.

Back in China, some inebriated poets who lived during the Tang Dynasty (618-907 CE) wrote poems hinting at independent Chinese distillation. In his verse, Buddhist poet Bai Juyi (772-846 CE) claimed to drink shaojiu, 'burnt alcohol'. Yong Tao, another drunken bard living in the same dynasty, penned a stanza which confessed Yong enjoyed the Chengdu region's offering of shaojiu so much, he never wanted to go home. But even at the most conservative estimate, Bai Juyi drank distillate just 26 years after Hayyan's death, which is no time at all considering it would be 400 years before Ramón Lull, who we'll meet later, was tinkering with a still in Europe. Around the 6th-7th century, a proto-spirit, formed by freezing fermented beverages, began appearing in China. The burn of the strong alcohol may have translated to 'burnt alcohol' in the poetry of these two drinkers (you never can tell with poets), but not necessarily.

It may refer to the distillation method used to create the distillate. The Silk Road, which began trade in the Han Dynasty (207-220 BCE), had long put distillation knowledge within reach of China. If distillation was present in China, it certainly wasn't widespread. Two accepted routes by which distillates became common are along the Silk Road in the Song Dynasty (960-1270 CE) or during the Mongolian Yuan Dynasty occupation (1271–1368 CE). An arguably more reliable source than the poets, a physiologist named Li Shizhen living in the Ming Dynasty (1368-1644 CE), believed distillation had been an import of the Mongol invasion in the previous dynasty.

The fusion of fermentation and distillation created a unique spirit. Baijiu, which translates as 'white alcohol', became popular among the peasant class. It was a cheaper alternative to the yellow wine of the elite, offering stronger impact for less money. As distillation technology spread, different provinces developed different methods. As such, baijius are as diverse in flavour as whole categories of spirit are from one another. Quantities of grain would alter, as would the composition of the qu. Ageing in porous earthenware jars became increasingly common as it was found this process mellowed pungency. Ceramic jars, much like wooden barrels, allow for oxygenation of the resting spirit, resulting in a smoother product. This was particularly important in such a highly alcoholic drink. Blending also became a mark of quality, with the best baijiu, much like cognac, being comprised of over 50 different pot-distilled spirits. These idiosyncrasies spread and mutated. Even through times of state-monopolised production, it was likely families would either slightly moderate technique, or keep their own secretly kindled.

MODERN SPIRIT WITH AN OLD HEART

The spirit developed fairly quietly in this way among the farming classes until the 20th century. Due to a state monopoly on alcohol production, there was little financial competition between producers, even if pride in technique existed. The state monopolies also did much to consolidate smaller businesses into larger factories. Come 1912, with the death of the Qing Dynasty and the end of imperial rule in China, this changed.

The entrepreneurial amongst baijiu producers saw an opportunity. 1915 saw both Moutai and Xinghuacun brands claim awards at the Pacific International Expo in San Francisco. However, their progress was slowed by civil war, beginning in 1927, and war against Japan in 1937. Any further progress as competitive businesses halted when the Chinese Communist Party took power in 1949. The CCP completely nationalised alcohol production. Although this had a large impact on individual businesses, the quality of alcohol went up as methods were recorded and standardised.

The rise of the Chinese Communist Party also had an interesting impact on the status of baijiu. It's leader, Mao Zedong, and his fellow officers toasted the formation of the People's Republic with a particular brand of baijiu. Premier Zhou Enlai took a shine to Kweichow Moutai's baijiu and in 1951 it became the official drink for Party banquets. The drink was soon associated with prestige and power. People began drinking baijiu in a completely different way. Gifts had always been important in Chinese society – especially alcohol. Wars had been waged over poor wine offerings. Baijiu became the ideal gift for business and social transactions. Political occasions were ceremoniously signed off with baijiu, notably the 1972 visit of Richard Nixon and more recently, during his term in office, Barack Obama.

Baijiu is still by far China's number one spirit and has dwarfed global sales of any other type of alcohol. For a long time, baijiu has been revered throughout China but little known in other parts of the world. A recent shift in awareness has seen the potent quintessence appearing on the backbars of many countries and bartenders experimenting with the spirit in cocktails. Baijiu looks to be expanding its markets indefinitely and this is reflected in giants such as Diageo, Pernod Ricard, LVMH (Louis Vuitton Moët Hennessy) and Thai Beverage all making eager acquisitions of some renowned producers. Baijiu's roots reach back thousands of years. Its strong, uncompromising flavour makes it stand out on the world stage. It will be exciting to see what the future holds for the godfather of spirits.

'The two of us drinking and wild flowers blooming
one cup another cup and still one more
I'm drunk and need to sleep and you're about to go
Tomorrow if you come again don't forget your zither.'

*A zither is a stringed instrument, the predecessor to a guitar.

THE BARTENDER'S
CHOICE

SPEED RAIL

HKB, Hong Kong Baijiu, 43%
This five-grain baijiu is definitely worth a go. The lower proof and sweetness makes it a lot more accessible. It smells like pear drops and ripe banana and has a flavour of poppy liqueur if you're acquainted.

BACK BAR

NUWA Red Star, 42%
A red sorghum baijiu with a light aromatic flavour. I took to this like a really full grappa, although my lady remains unconvinced. It's big flavour all the way, but the lower proof makes it an enjoyable sipper (for some).

TOP SHELF

Kweichow Moutai, 53%

If you've enjoyed the journey down the rabbit hole so far, by all means... charge on. Though tasty in its own right, I would not recommend starting your baijiu journey with Moutai. This sauce-aroma baijiu made with sorghum hails from Maotai, China's most famous distilling town. Typical soy flavours and a fine expression offer notes similar to a decent porter – cacao and coffee.

3 WAYS
TO DRINK
BAIJIU

TRANS-SIBERIAN EXPRESS

25ml HKB Hong Kong
Baijiu
25ml vodka
25ml lemon juice
25ml sugar syrup
(1:1 water:sugar)

› Begin chilling coupe glass
› Add all ingredients and shake hard for
   12-15 seconds
› Discard ice in coupe and double strain
   into glass
› Garnish with lemon twist (squeeze with
   skin side facing into drink)

RED AND GOLD NEGRONI

20ml baijiu
(NU WA Red Star)
25ml Bigalett China-
China liqueur
25ml Cocchi Vermouth
di Torino

› Add all ingredients to mixing glass
› Add ice and stir till tasty
› Strain into rocks glass
› Add fresh ice and garnish with orange peel

BAIJIU BIJOU

20ml HKB Hong Kong
Baijiu
20ml green Chartreuse
10ml Suze
10ml Lillet Blanc
2 dashes orange bitters

The sweet funky pear on this lower
strength (43%) baijiu plays wonderfully
with the herbs and bitters of the other
ingredients.

› Begin chilling coupe
› Add all ingredients to mixing glass
› Add ice and stir till tasty
› Discard ice in coupe and strain into glass

'I think if we drink enough Moutai,
we can solve anything.'

(Said to president Deng Xiaoping,
during a diplomatic visit)

HENRY
KISSINGER

CURIOSITIES

The word *ganbei*, meaning dry cup, is similar to 'cheers' in English. It is often said when drinking a toast at a meal. Much etiquette surrounds giving toasts, including reciprocating a toast to someone who has toasted you. Thankfully, being drunk in the company of a host isn't rude in China; it is considered a sign of hospitality received.

The buying culture around rare baijius rivals that of rare whiskies. In 2010 a rare bottle of 1958 Moutai sold for 1.45 million yuan (around £140,000). The reason for such a high price in spite of age was that China had suffered a grain shortage at the time of production, which made baijiu very scarce.

If there's ever a booze scare China's the place to go. In 2012 estimates have it that there was well over double the amount of baijiu produced than vodka.

COGNAC

The story of the birth of cognac is a tale as laden with misfortune as it is with good luck. Though brandy is common around the globe, none is more famous than cognac. Fascinatingly, both fortune and disaster contributed to the rise of one of the most globally lauded spirits. It took billions of years to make a soil uniquely beneficial to certain species of grape, and since then cognac has seen all manner of tribulation and victory. The bloodshed of opposed religious ideologies, famine and plagues, devastating both people and vine, have all played their part in the making of cognac. It is testament to the spirit of this aged scion that in the face of all its trials, cognac has not only survived but thrived.

WHAT IS COGNAC?

Cognac is a type of brandy. Brandy is made from distilling the fermented juice, skins, or seeds of fruits. In the case of cognac, this ferment comes from the juice of grapes. Cognac must be made of at least 90% ugni blanc (the most common grape in cognac), folle blanche, colombard, or a blend of those varieties. It can only be made within the region of Cognac, which is made up of Crus. There are six Crus in Cognac, differentiated by their soil quality. From the most highly regarded soil to the least the Crus are called: Grande Champagne, Petite Champagne, Borderies, Fins Bois, Bons Bois and Bois Ordinaires. Cognacs are usually

blends consisting of different ages and Crus. Blended cognac is often made from different Crus but can come from the same region, known as a single Cru. Blends of between 20-60 aged spirits aren't uncommon. If the cognac consists of a blend of spirits solely between the Grand and Petit Champagne regions, the cognac may be called 'fine champagne'. The most common age statements of cognacs are: VS, 'very special', where the youngest spirits in the bottle have to have been aged for at least two years; VSOP, 'very special old pale', in which the youngest spirits must have been aged at least four years; and XO 'extra old' cognac, in which the youngest spirit in the bottle must be no fewer than ten years old*.

*The 'minimum age' for XO was increased from six to ten years in 2018.

A BRIEF HISTORY OF WINE & WINE GODS

Around 7-8,000 years ago the domestication of one of the most culturally important fruits began. Thought to have first been cultivated in Middle Eastern Georgia, the grape genus *Vitis vinifera* spread through surrounding countries. Wine jugs dating from around 5400-5000 BCE have been unearthed in Iran. Over time, the tradition of winemaking became more sophisticated. Egyptian and Greek civilisations acknowledged the merits of aged wine – a tradition continued 3,000 years on when cognac emerged. Gods were worshipped in association with wine and drinking and none were more synonymous with wine than Dionysius.

Worshipped later by the Romans under the name of Bacchus, Dionysius was heralded as far back as 1500 BCE as god of fertility and wine.

The wine god was conceived during an affair between Zeus and his mortal lover Semele. Zeus' jealous wife Hera tricked a pregnant Semele into making Zeus reveal himself to Semele in his true form. This burnt Semele to death. A foetal Dionysius survived and was sewn into Zeus' thigh to continue gestation. Following Dionysius' birth, Hera was still scorned over the betrayal. She had a young Dionysius torn apart by Titans. Resurrected by Rhea, Dionysius was sent to grow up safely among the nymphs. This resurrection mirrored the life cycle of grapevines, which withered in the cold months and returned in the spring.

Nowadays there are just under 80 species of grape that grow in Asia, Europe and the Americas. From these species there are over 10,000 grape varieties. In France alone, there are some 1,300 varieties of grape made from various species (including hybrids, which occur when one species is grafted onto another by grape growers in order to marry favourable qualities).

THE FINEST SPOT FOR EAU-DE-VIE

The city of Cognac is situated along the limestone-rich banks of the River Charente, which flows northwest into the Atlantic from an estuary near Rochefort. The pure water from the river later diluted strong eau-de-vie, the water of life. Well before brandies were tasted, the location offered great trading routes for the region's highly reputed salt, which was famed as far back as 430 CE for its preservative powers.

The warm weather was also ideal for grape growing. Over centuries a grape variety known as colombard became popular, thanks to its alcoholic strength and sweet flavour once fermented.

'It is well to remember that there are five reasons for drinking: the arrival of a friend, one's present or future thirst, the excellence of the cognac, or any other reason.'

W . ☾ .

FIELDS

By the 1100s, La Rochelle had become an indispensable trading station for wines, but trade wasn't always smooth. Despite optimum environmental factors, other conditions hindered progress. English rule of Aquitaine between 1154-1453 CE often created tension between the two nations. During periods of fighting, vineyards were often destroyed. The outbreak of the Black Death, which swept over Europe between 1348-1445 CE, wiped out significant numbers of the French population. Grape growers killed by the epidemic left their unattended crops to perish. War and disease would continue to surround the development of a spirit soon to find world renown.

Whilst English-French relations were disturbing the vintners of the Charente region, Ramón Lull, one of the earliest evidenced distillers of aqua vitae, was hard at work. Born in Muslim-ruled Majorca in the early 1230s, Lull's religious quest compelled him to learn both Latin and Arabic. By the end of his life, Lull had, through his exploration of Arabic texts, uncovered the secrets of distillation and applied his findings to wine, making some of Europe's first documented eau-de-vie. Between 1274-75, Lull was summoned to Montpellier where he may have crossed paths with another Arabic scholar, Doctor Arnaldo de Villanova, who began to promote eau-de-vie as a medicine. This places the emergence of spirits in France around the latter half of the 13th Century. Given how Lull and missionary monks travelled, news quickly spread of the life-giving elixir, and before long, the secrets of eau-de-vie trickled down to those outside of the church.

In 1494, king-to-be François I was born in Cognac. This royal relationship would see eau-de-vie from the area enjoy significant tax breaks. By the mid-1550s the Charente region was exporting a prized wine, preferred in the Low Countries because of its sweetness. Coastal vintners had taken to planting vines bearing less flavourful grapes than the colombard cépagne. Paradoxically, though the colombard grapes made a fine wine of high strength, they produced a lesser eau-du-vie. The choice wine, which became known as vin du Cognac, was transported with the coastal eau-du-vies on Dutch merchant vessels from Rochefort and neighbouring La Rochelle.

The Dutch would do a great deal for cognac over the years. Dutch settlers conducted much of the distillation in the ports along the west coast. During the late 1500s, as they sold the wine with eau-de-vie from neighbouring regions, traders from the Netherlands helped propagate the idea that Cognac sold fine produce. The Dutch often sold French eau-de-vie as *brandewijn* or burnt wine, which would eventually become the word 'brandy'.

SUCCESS IN THE FACE OF ADVERSITY

The French Wars of Religion between 1562-1598 created tensions between crown-favoured Catholics and Protestant Huguenots, which would last for centuries. Even during these wars, the largely Protestant Charente region still made progress. An early inland adopter, eager to join in on the coast's successful spirit trade, was Jehan Serazin. In 1571 he set up one of the first known distilleries in the Charente area as the *merchand et faizeur d'eau-de-vie*. An influx of entrepreneurial Dutch traders married into Charente families and began eau-de-vie production, capitalising on the positions of port towns along the Charente. By the 1620s, in spite of the religious discontent both in France and the Netherlands (which had already fought 50 years of the Eighty Years War) La Rochelle was a thriving metropolis of trade.

Back in Charente the first trading houses began forming. Some of these became the bases of power, which survived an almost constant onslaught of problems. One such house, established by Phillipe Augier in 1643, weathered 370 years of tribulations only to be bought out by Pernod-Ricard in 2013. Through the latter half of the 17th century, there were many triumphs in the midst of difficulties. The Fronde Rebellion occurred between 1648-52. It saw most Protestants in Charente rise up against Catholic rule. Interestingly, Cognac was one of the few places that didn't rebel. It was rewarded with tax exemption.

Come 1678, 'Cogniacke' was on the lips of the English, but cognac production would be disrupted in 1685, when it became illegal to be Protestant in France. Many Protestant traders of the Charente fled, seeking asylum in countries such as the Netherlands or Britain. A million more Huguenots were trapped in France, facing potential death were their beliefs discovered. Yet even this proved advantageous for cognac's reputation. Whilst abroad, Charente Protestants would promote the eau-de-vie of their region. Low supplies of cognac due to a loss of workforce served to increase demand. By the 1720s, though most cognacs were still sold colourless, some began to carry the gold hue of age, in part to compete with new rum and gin markets.

The years drew on. Colonial defeats in the 1750s left the French economy in disarray, although rising cognac sales offered some relief. The 1700s saw an influx of Irish and English settlers to the Charente region, intent on joining a growing eau-de-vie trade. Some of these names are still famous today. Richard Hennessey, hailing from County Cork, founded his distillery in 1765. Thomas Hine from Dorset, England, married into a family that owned a distillery. When his father-in-law died in the 1790s, Hine took over production. He later named the company after himself and laid lasting foundations for a family dynasty.

REFINEMENT, GEOLOGY & PROSPERITY

After a drop in sales due to naval blockades in the Napoleonic wars, by 1819 83% of cognac being produced was exported to Britain. Moreover, barrels that had languished in cellars throughout the war now emerged all the richer for their age. In Britain, these fine spirits were dubbed as 'Napoleonic brandy'. The rise in brandy consumption was curtailed by an 1826 tax on French imports by the British government. This slowed short-term sales but did much for cognac's prestige. Robert Peel reduced the levy in the 1840s and by the end of the decade cognac sales soared. Fortuitously, this fruitful time coincided with the decision of whether to use Aeneas Coffey's continuous still. 1791 already saw cognac houses band together for quality control, indicative of a similar pride to the Irish in regards to distillation techniques. The fact cognac houses were doing so well in the 1850s meant there wasn't much to consider. The 1850s also saw numerous imitations of cognac appear on markets, but one man's research at this time came to offer a completely new definition of cognac, distinguishing it from fakes.

Henri Coquand was a professor in geology who was interested in the *terroir* of Cognac and how it related to the spirit made there. He took it upon himself to roam the area on his horse, accompanied by a *dégustateur* (a taster of spirits). As he examined soil samples, he made predictions about the differences in taste each type of soil would produce. Lo and behold, when the cognac taster returned from the cellars, Coquand's predictions proved to be accurate. By 1858 a map was drawn up depicting areas in response to Coquand's findings.

THE DEATH OF VINES

Phylloxera are near-microscopic insects that feed on the roots of vulnerable vines. The early 1870s saw the introduction of the pest from America. Phylloxera ravaged the grapes of France, which had no resistance to these small relatives of the aphid family. By 1880, vineyards in the south of France were decimated. Between the years 1875 and 1900 nearly half of French viniculture would be affected, Cognac included. Slow to acknowledge the scale of the problem, the state reward for a solution jumped from 20,000 francs in 1870 to 300,000 francs in 1874.

In 1873 botanist Jules Émile Planchon travelled to America, believing the country to be the source of the pox. In New York he met Charles Riley, an entomologist, and together they compiled a list of vines resistant to phylloxera, which included *Vitis rupestris*, *Vitis riparia*, and *Vitis berlanieri*. The former two vines, when grafted with the Old World stock in Cognac, suffered from chlorosis. The roots were unaccustomed to the high concentration of chalk. The vines wilted, yellowed and died, the grapes with them. Phylloxera persisted plaguing Cognac vines.

In 1887 Pierre Viala made a similar trip to America. He met with a luminary vintner named Thomas Munson, who'd already explored much Texan land, prodigious in his thirst for grape knowledge. Munson led Viala to *Vitis berlanieri* once more, which was both resistant to phylloxera and grew well in the chalky soil of Cognac. In honour of Munson's efforts, Denison in Texas and Cognac became sister cities.

THE 20TH CENTURY AND BEYOND

The first decade of the 20th century was a turning point for cognac. Finally over the hardships of phylloxera, houses started creating their own blends. In 1936 the reputation of cognac became acknowledged by law as it was protected against impersonators by an Appellation d'Origine Contrôlée. Eventually the ugni blanc grape became championed over the folle blanche and colombard varieties. It was robust against frost and many felt the bland grape was a finer conduit for imparting the flavour of Limousin oak barrels. With the exception of war-induced fluctuations due to a depleted work force or high export tariffs, cognac experienced steady growth and expansion until the 1970s, when a series of trade wars saw a marked decline in sales. Trade finally stabilised in the 1990s, and successes in Chinese and Japanese markets provided a boost to the industry.

Cognac has always been good at facing adversity. Even now, cognac houses are repositioning their XO category, extending age restrictions from six years to ten in order to further appeal to a market of connoisseurs. Cognac also, despite coming from such a small area, enjoys a surprisingly large and diverse fan base. From the old-boy clubs of London's West End to the hip-hop clubs of Brooklyn and beyond, its phenomenal popularity pervades myriad cultures. Jay-Z even partly owns a brand of VSOP cognac called D'USSÉ. The American rap scene seems to have adopted this aristocratic spirit as its own, but cognac's popularity extends far beyond rap circles. The USA consumes the most cognac in the world but China has also come to develop a strong relationship with the spirit. Both Chinese and North American drinkers drink cognac in bars and clubs. Unlike Americans, who also drink cognac at home, the Chinese prefer to drink at social banquets as part of business transactions or for celebratory occasions. Fitting with the cultural tradition of guanxi, which means the cultivation of relationships with others, expensive bottles are bought to be presented to business associates, friends or family. Funnily enough, in Cognac itself, the locals enjoy the spirit in a way that would seem sacrilegious to most cognac aficionados, accompanied with tonic. Perseverance and a constant strive for quality from producers has made cognac an aristocrat of the spirits industry. Because of this, cognac will certainly continue to hold its place as one of the world's very finest spirits.

THE BARTENDER'S
CHOICE

SPEED RAIL

Courvoisier VS, 40%

This is generally my go-to cognac for mixing.
It's got a decent body, which holds up well in
cocktails due to its richness, strength
and balance.

BACK BAR

H by Hine VSOP, 40%

A delicious fine champagne sip from the Hine
house. Somehow remains powerful whilst still
being smooth.

TOP SHELF

A.E. Dor Fine Champagne Cognac, 40%
Really special after dinner sipper here. Warm the glass in your hands after a hearty meal. Please don't mix it with anything except good company.

3 WAYS
TO DRINK
COGNAC

FOGCUTTER

20ml cognac
20ml gin
20ml gold rum
25ml pineapple juice
25ml lemon juice
12.5ml orgeat syrup
12.5ml amontillado
sherry (float)

The original calls for orange juice, but I've never quite been able to resist this version with pineapple.

› Add all ingredients (except sherry) to shaker
› Shake as hard as possible for 12-15 seconds
› Double strain into brandy glass and fill with crushed ice
› Pour on sherry float and garnish with pineapple leaf

VIEUX CARRÉ

20ml VSOP cognac
20ml rye
20ml Cocchi Vermouth
di Torino
7.5ml Bénédictine
2 dashes Peychaud's
bitters
2 dashes Angostura
bitters

With a name meaning 'old square' in French, this drink is a siren's call to New Orleans. Reputedly invented in the Hotel Monteleone – frequented by the likes of William Faulkner, Truman Capote and Tennessee Williams.

› Add all ingredients to a mixing glass
› Add cubed ice and stir till diluted to taste
› Strain into a rocks glass and add fresh ice
› Garnish with chunky orange twist

SNAKEBITE

20ml cognac
20ml calvados
20ml Żubrówka Bison
Grass vodka
25ml lemon juice
15ml beer syrup* (I used
King Cobra)
1 egg white
2 dashes Peychaud's
bitters

› Begin chilling cocktail coupe

› Add all ingredients to shaker

› Dry shake to emulsify the egg white

› Wet shake hard for 12-15 seconds

› Discard ice in coupe and double strain
  into glass

› Garnish with two drops of Peychaud's to
  look like a 'bite'

*Reduce beer to 1/3 original amount by heating on low
heat. Allow to cool. Dissolve white sugar into liquid at a
ratio of 1:1.

'Claret is the liquor for boys; port, for men; but he who aspires to be a hero must drink brandy.'

SAMUEL
JOHNSON

'Is that Lucifer juice in that two cup he sippin'?
That's D'USSÉ baby welcome
to the dark side.'

JAY
Z

CURIOSITIES

The Grande and Petite Champagne regions of Cognac are called such because 'champagne' is an archaic French term for countryside – the area has nothing to do with the sparkling wine. The word 'champagne' in the rural context has since developed into the similar 'campagne'.

The cognac market relies heavily on exportation for business. A staggering 93% of cognac is sold outside of France. In fact, the sales of scotch whisky in France over one month are greater than the amount of cognac sold in the country over the course of a year.

The Limousin oak trees, which produce the barrels cognac is aged in, were planted to replace the many hundreds of thousands of trees cut down to build a significant French naval fleet in the 1660s. The purpose of the fleet was to protect ships loaded with trade cargo, such as eau-de-vie.

VODKA

Even if you're not a vodka drinker, the absence of vodka in a bar anywhere in the world might be an arresting sight. But it's only relatively recently, after rich historical centuries in Slavic countries, that vodka emerged ubiquitous on the world stage. Once in global favour it became one of the most popular spirits on the planet. But behind vodka's perpetual popularity are contrasting stories depending on which country's history you visit. From monopolised drug to important cultural binding agent, vodka has been the symbol of both hospitality and hostility. When making vodka, producers aspire to make the purest distillate possible through refinement and the removal of impurities. In many ways, vodka's history reflects the spirit in which it is made.

WHAT IS VODKA?

Vodka is made by distilling the ferment of raw agricultural materials. Generally, commercial vodkas are distilled from grains such as wheat or rye, or potatoes. However, throughout history vodkas have been made from nearly every product imaginable. Producers regularly turn to a variety of different fruit, vegetables or grains, ranging from rice to quinoa and sugar beet.

Vodka is almost always rectified to remove impurities. These multiple distillations extract congers from the distillate to get as close to pure ethanol as possible. The 'heads' and tails' of distilled alcohol are undesirable substances, which evaporate

at different temperatures to ethanol's boiling point of 78.37 °C. Post-distillation, the vodka more often than not is filtered. The majority of producers filter their vodka with activated charcoal. But with the ever-present idiosyncrasies of the booze world everything from coconut husks, quartz crystals, specialised filter paper and diamonds are in use. In order to lower the alcohol volume, as with other alcohols, producers cut the distillate with water. Since vodka is bottled unaged, only the raw matter it's fermented from, the purity of the distillate and the water used to cut it determines its flavour profile. Some producers tap various geo-specific water sources in the name of purity, including mountain springs, volcanic lava fields and limestone-rich wells. These sources may be further purified if the producer is not fully satisfied with the water.

RYE & DISTILLATION THROUGH CHRISTIAN EUROPE

Rye, categorised as *Secale cereale*, is a type of grass and member of the cereal family. Indigenous to Eastern Turkey, rye is thought to have been first cultivated around 1800-1500 BCE. It was initially an unfavourable crop, producing a much more bitter flour than its wheat or barley counterparts. However, because of its ability to grow in adverse weather conditions, persevering in snow if sunlight could bring the plant's temperature above freezing, it became a staple crop in colder climes. Adopted along the grain belt, which runs through Poland and Ukraine, across Belarus, Lithuania, Latvia and Estonia into Russia, the crop played a vital part in sustaining these countries.

Until strong spirits arrived in Eastern Europe, most had to content themselves with beers, usually made from rye or mead produced from honey. 1405 offers the first mention of Polish spirit. It is possible reality reflects records and that the Polish were distilling aqua vitae before the Russians, since Poland is closer than Russia to Italy, where much distillation knowledge came from.

By the late 1430s delegates were sent from Moscow to the Italian Ecumenical Councils of the Catholic Church. These representatives visited Florence and Venice, where they would surely have been introduced to aqua vitae, if they didn't already have knowledge of the medicinal elixir. However the secret of distilling found its way to the Muscovite courts, by the 1470s it must have become such a part of Muscovy society that production was restricted. Prince Ivan III decreed that the state would hold monopoly on spirit production, with sole exemption given to the Orthodox Church.

Fortunately for the Poles, their ruler took a different view. In 1546, King Jan Olbracht granted permission that any of his subjects might distil freely, on the provision they paid tax. From the offset, vodkas were typically produced with surplus grain-barley, oats and wheat, but by far the most common ingredient was rye. Potatoes were introduced to Europe from Peru in the 1500s. Whilst potatoes were probably used in a pinch from their introduction, their use didn't become common practice for vodka making in Poland until the 1750s. The trend never quite took off in Russia.

In Russia and Poland, from the appearance of the very first spirits, the distillates were flavoured with herbs, berries, honey or spices. In part this was telling of people's association with the elixirs as medicine. But the flavourings were also to make the drinks more palatable. This aim took another incarnation, to remove as many impurities from the distillate as possible. In pursuit of this purity, distillers conducted numerous distillations (far more than other alcohol producers of the time) and subjected the resultant distillates to all manner of filtration.

In 1547 Ivan the Terrible became the first self-proclaimed tsar of Russia at 16. Conversely to his Polish counterpart, he instated laws whereby vodka, already solely produced by the state, could only be served in state taverns. Vodka played a great role in his personal as well as public affairs. His adolescence of drinking strong spirit before heading off with friends to assault peasants and rape girls didn't bode well. Thankfully, Ivan turned a corner when crowned, in marrying Anastasia, who seemed to have a calming influence on the tsar. It wasn't

to last. The princess died in what Ivan saw as suspicious circumstances. He took solace in vodka and soon returned to his violent ways. Those lucky enough to have the pleasure of Ivan's company at court sometimes refused to accompany the prince in his drinking towards oblivion. They were subjected to threats of torture and death.

THE GREAT DRINKING PRINCE PETER

One hundred years on from Ivan, in the 1680s, another Russian prince, Peter, not yet out of his teens, could be found taking breakfast with a pint of vodka and a bottle of sherry. Later, while travelling across Europe under a pseudonym between 1697-98 with an entourage of 250 ambassadors, Peter would often run up monumental drinking tabs. Take a morning welcomed by a bottle of brandy and a bottle of sherry,

'I began to think vodka was my drink at last...
It went straight down into my stomach like a
sword swallower's sword and made me feel
powerful and godlike.'

SYLVIA
PLATH

followed by eight bottles of wine to help the day pass. In addition to letting his royal hosts accommodate the expense of such luxuries, he would exasperate them with his antics. Visiting William III in 1697, Peter succeeded in enraging the King of England. His favoured monkey, which kept the tsar company by perching on his chair back while he drank and dined, took offence to the king and attacked him.

In spite of his prodigious drinking, Peter managed to enact a series of systematic modernisations. He developed naval fleets, having acquired knowledge from experienced Dutch and British officers. Similarly, he adopted scientific research and ideas on governing in an attempt to forward his country. His drinking then, was only rivalled by his work ethic, and though he partied endlessly, he also seemed to work just as

tirelessly. His band of thirsty companions, picked mostly for their drinking abilities, became known as the 'All-Mad, All-Drunken, All-Jesting Assembly'. The group even had a rather elaborate code with punitive measures. Among these was the Great Eagle – a 1.5-litre vessel taken up in two hands. Should you incur the punishment, the Great Eagle would be filled with vodka and the guilty party had to drink up.

VODKA BY NAME & CLARITY REFINED

The infancy of ardent spirit in the Russian royal court may not have been the most dignified affair. Over two to three hundred years, the tone ranged from deeply disturbing to hilarious. The name 'vodka', derived from the Slavic word for water, voda, certainly reflected this attitude. Anyone who's read a Tolstoy novel will know how many affectionate names Russians can grant one person. Vodka is a diminutive version of *voda*, but far from connoting 'less than' water, it is an address of endearment, like saying 'little love'. The first record of vodka being referred to as such is in 1751 when Tsarina Elizabeth I put forward a decree entitled 'Who is to be Permitted to Possess Vats for the Distillation of Vodka'.

It seems that having acquired a name, vodka enjoyed a coming of age, which offered reprieve from its past. Catherine the Great was a shrewd promoter of Russian culture. In 1765 she revised the state monopoly for the production of vodka, allowing families of the Russian elite to begin distilling their own grain spirit for the first time. The effect was competitiveness between distillery houses, which served to produce some of the finest Russian vodka yet made. Pleased, proud and eager to promote the achievements of Russian ingenuity to the world, she began sending samples of this exemplary Russian vodka to the luminaries and blue bloods of Europe. Immanuel Kant, Johann Wolfgang Goethe, Voltaire, Gustave III of Sweden and Prussia's Frederick the Great were all recipients and admirers of Russia's pure spirit. In the 1770s Carl Linnaeus, the naturalist responsible for devising how we categorise living organisms, found Russian vodka to have a 'magical power'. It is fascinating to reflect that despite these prominent figures becoming enraptured with vodka, the drink didn't find much of a market until the 1900s.

REVOLUTION, EXILE & THE SEDATIVE OF THE PEOPLE

The Napoleonic wars, which waged from 1803-1815, saw Russian soldiers posted in stations across Europe. Where the Russian soldiers went, vodka followed. Whereas particular alcohols tended to catch on in Europe, such as brandy or scotch, vodka never really took off. This may have been due to vodka's neutral flavour profile – the tastes of other soldiers having grown accustomed to the stronger flavours of brandy, gin or rum.

In the 1860s one Piotr Smirnov opened a vodka distillery that would eventually go on to infiltrate global markets. But the journey wouldn't be easy. The new vodka boasted charcoal filtration, numerous distillations and was purported to be free of impurities. Smirnov's vodka soon found favour among the Romanov Court and Piotr passed on a hopeful legacy to his son Vladimir. Vladimir, however, would have less luck than his father. By 1914 the state banned production.

Though 1917 saw the Bolsheviks, led by Lenin, overthrow the monarchy in the October Revolution, the party continued the ban on vodka. Lenin believed alcohol was a state agent of control, produced to stupefy the masses. A state-wide prohibition on alcohol ensued and Vladimir managed to narrowly escape capture and death. Finding himself exiled in Constantinople, modern day Turkey, he took what resources he had and attempted to restore the business. Failing here, Vladimir moved to France, once again trying to revive the business. He sought a French audience, changing the company name to Ste. Pierre Smirnoff Fils, but the business couldn't gain traction. At a loss, Vladimir went on to sell the company to Rudolf Kunett. Kunett, unfortunately, chose to open a distillery in the USA, which would, in 1920, embark on its Great Experiment. Anticipating little success, Rudolf sold the business on a 5% retainer per bottle to Heublein. The company would go on to have minor success in the 40s with the invention of the Moscow mule cocktail, a mix of vodka, ginger beer and lime. Smirnoff's great triumph wouldn't come about until Sean Connery played 007 in the 1962 film *Dr No*.

Interestingly enough, once Stalin succeeded as the leader of the Soviet Communist party, he once again began production of vodka, against what would have been Lenin's wishes. What is even more fascinating is that he upped the strength of vodka to some 50% ABV. This not only conflicted in principle with the ideology of Lenin, but also went against the better judgement of Dmitri Mendeleev. In 1893 Mendeleev had concluded, having been the state-appointed director of the Imperial Bureau of Weights and Measures, that the optimum ratio for spirit

to water was 38% to 62%. Since calculators were a far-off invention, the ratio was amended to 40% spirit to 60% water, for simplicity of tax. It is no great coincidence that the general alcoholic content of spirits globally falls into these margins, but Stalin chose to ignore Mendeleev's observations. Carl Marx famously wrote, 'religion is the opium of the people'; in a similar manner, it seems Stalin viewed vodka as the sedative of the Russians.

Prohibition did nothing good for vodka's reputation in America. What was labelled as 'vodka' on American shores was infinitely removed from the pure spirit distilled in Russia. The Second World War undoubtedly had a profound impact on how vodka drinkers were viewed. A drink that had only recently entered Western Europe's sphere of consciousness became associated with perpetually plastered Russians who were supplied with vodka throughout the war. Though their effectiveness went seemingly unscathed, their lowered inhibitions caused other problems. It is estimated over two million women were raped by Russian soldiers as the Soviet army marched on Berlin.

PROOF OF STRENGTH

Eventually vodka's popularity in Europe caught on. People were enticed by a drink that couldn't be smelt on the breath. By 1975 Stateside, vodka had outshone whiskey, rum and tequila to become America's most popular spirit. First launched in New York in 1979, the Absolut brand of vodka revolutionised not only vodka sales but alcohol marketing in general. The brand paired with eminent artists such as Andy Warhol and created a cool and cosmopolitan image for its consumers. Mikael Gorbachev,

final leader of the Communist party, chose to shut down vodka production in 1985. He thought wine and beer might be a preferable option to neat vodka, which had caused a host of health and social problems. Just like American prohibition, the result was loss of revenue and social unrest. The law was quickly repealed in 1987.

Today vodka is one of most widely drunk spirits produced and manages to cater for every budget and class. Super-premium vodkas sell for exceptional prices, whereas the low-end expressions tend to be some of the cheapest spirits available. Vodka has a dual personality. In one sense, it can be perceived as the epitome of refinement with important cultural implications. In another, it is a numbing agent, capable of being personally and socially destructive. For those with less of a palate for more characterful spirits, vodka can be anything they want it to be. As such, vodka is often popular with younger drinkers. Its neutral profile also means it mixes easily without overpowering delicate ingredients. However, connoisseurs increasingly seek character in their vodka, including mouthfeel as much as flavour. Vodka's rise to global prominence in such a short time makes it arguably the quickest and most widely adopted spirit. This omnipresence makes vodka's impact as clear as the spirit itself.

THE BARTENDER'S
CHOICE

SPEED RAIL

Wyborowa, 40%

Whilst Russian brands would have you believe rye is the best crop for producing vodka, my personal preference is actually potato. I often stock this Polish brand on bars I run. For the price it's great quality, and I find it has a fuller mouthfeel than some of its grain counterparts in the same class.

BACK BAR

Żubrówka Bison Grass Vodka, 40%

Not all vodkas are flavourless. Żubrówka is fantastically versatile and a fine example of a traditional flavoured vodka. The herbaceous notes play wonderfully with everything from gin to calvados. Well worth keeping a bottle round to play with.

TOP SHELF

Silver Tree Small Batch, 40%

In trying to confront my own snobbery on
believing you shouldn't pay more than £25 for
a bottle of vodka, I happened across this.
A superb blend of summer wheat, potato
and malted barley.

3WAYS
TO DRINK
VODKA

ESPRESSO MARTINI

The late great Dick Bradsell's most popular creation. Famously fixed up for a customer in the Soho Brasserie when she requested a drink that would, 'wake me up and fuck me up.' I'm certain she wasn't disappointed.

50ml vodka
25ml coffee liqueur
(Kaluha foams pretty well, however, less sweet liqueurs may need a dash or two of sugar syrup)
Double shot of fresh espresso

› Add all ingredients to shaker
› Shake with all your might for 12-15 seconds – you want a really foamy drink

VESPER MARTINI

30ml London dry gin
20ml vodka
10ml Cocchi Americano

This is the first martini James Bond orders in Ian Fleming's *Casino Royale*. He names the drink after his love interest. Wonderfully delicate and balanced, it's a lovely pre-dinner sip. Careful not to over dilute it!

› Begin chilling cocktail coupe
› Add all ingredients into a mixing glass
› Add ice to the very top
› Stir until sufficiently chilled and diluted
› Discard ice in coupe and strain the drink into the coupe
› Garnish with lemon twist (from a height and distance is best – remember the drink is delicate)

WINTER ROSE

40ml Żubrówka vodka
20ml Cocchi Vermouth
di Torino
7.5ml Fernet Branca
3 dashes orange bitters

This drink is a variation on a delicious off-the-menu drink I had at The Blind Pig in Soho, London. It was called the Rose Field and utilised Chase Marmalade Vodka to great effect. This version uses herbaceous Żubrówka instead.

› Add all ingredients to mixing glass
› Fill with ice and stir till sufficiently chilled and diluted
› Strain into rocks glass and add fresh ice
› Express oils of orange peel over drink and garnish with rosemary spring

'Alcohol is the anesthesia
by which we endure the operation of life.'

GEORGE
BERNARD SHAW

'No, bo wodka stygnie!'
(Hey, the vodka is getting cold!)

POLISH
TOAST

CURIOSITIES

After a drunken coming of age, Leo Tolstoy renounced vodka as poison. He became an active temperance campaigner and turned his capacities as a writer to temperance literature, including an 1890 piece called *Why Do Men Stupefy Themselves?*

In Poland alone, it is estimated there are over 1,000 brands of vodka. Add those to the expressions produced in Russia and Scandinavia and you'll have your work cut out picking a favourite!

Traditionally, in Russia each new round of drinks means a new toast. Toasts are often elaborate anecdotal stories. At formal occasions there is also a procedure to which toast is for what – at a birthday for example, the first toast is to the person whose birthday it is, the second to the parents, etc.

SCOTCH & IRISH WHISKIES

Whereas its trans-Atlantic children bourbon and rye conjure images of bar brawls and bawdiness, there are fewer greater symbols of refinement in our culture than a glass of scotch. A stone's throw away from Scotland, a more rebellious nation was busy crafting its own whiskey. Irish whiskey was, in certain parts of history, one of the world's most popular spirits. Without the Irish invention of the Coffey still, shunned by its countrymen but adopted by the Scottish, the spirits industry and the tale of whisky might be very different. The history of scotch and Irish whiskey is as nuanced as the secrets that occur in barrels during maturation. Their legacies and influence have instilled lasting traditions spanning continents.

WHAT IS SCOTCH?

Scotch is whisky produced in Scotland. There are two different types of scotch. The first and most prestigious is malt whisky, distilled from 100% malted barley. Malting is the process by which the grain begins to germinate while being soaked in water. Drying the malt with warm air then stops germination. This partial germination produces sugars, starches and enzymes essential to the production of alcohol. The malt is batch-distilled twice (sometimes more), in copper pot stills. The whisky-producing areas of Scotland are divided into regions: Lowlands, Highlands,

Islands, Campbeltown, Speyside and Islay. Single-malt scotch is the end produce of one distillery, whereas blended malts marry characteristics from the single malts of different distilleries to enhance their flavour. Blends may also be made from the second type of scotch, grain whisky. Grain whisky is made using malted barley but can contain other malted or unmalted grains or cereals. Grain whisky is made through continuous distillation and is often used for blending as the production method yields far greater quantities than batch distillation. Some grain whiskies are, however, bottled unblended. Grain whisky bottled from a single distillery is known as single grain. Scotch is aged on average between 3-12 years but some are aged for 50 years or more and sell for tens of thousands of pounds. The age statement on a bottle of scotch has to be a declaration of the youngest whisky in the bottling.

AND IRISH WHISKEY?

Irish whiskey has different types, much like scotch, but these are split into malt, pot still, grain and blended. The first and most prestigious is malt whisky, distilled from 100% malted barley. In a pot still whiskey, there is a minimum of 30% malted and 30% unmalted barley with a maximum of 5% other grains or cereals – it must also be distilled in a pot still and can only come from one distillery. Grain whiskey is made using a maximum of 30% of malted barley and is produced using continuous distillation. Similarly to scotch, grain whiskey from a single distillery can be bottled and sold as single grain or used in blends. Blended whiskey is made from a mixture of two or more of any other style.

TO 'E' OR NOT TO 'E'?

The two spellings of whisk(e)y come down to reputation. In

the later 1800s when Ireland's whiskey far outclassed Scotland on the world stage, the Irish chose to use the 'e' to distinguish themselves from the Scottish counterparts. On emigration, Irish immigrants took that 'e' with them. Other countries such as Canada and Japan chose not to adopt the letter – presumably to position themselves alongside scotch, which had by then become far more popular than Irish whiskey.

A DISTILLER'S DREAM

Cereal grain cultivation for use in fermentation has a lineage of some 10,000 years, reaching Europe from the Fertile Crescent around 6000 BCE. Among the cereals commonly turned into alcohol, barley is, from an alcohol producer's perspective, the king. Robust against corruption from moisture and bacteria because of a protective shell, the crop is easily malted. The malting process begins deconstruction of the grain

and releases enzymes vital for turning starch to fermentable sugars. Wheat, rye and oats were often susceptible to bacterial adulteration without the technologies of modernity to monitor their malting. In Ireland and Scotland, the malt was often dried with burning peat, which some distilleries still do today. The peat imparts a smoky flavour to the whisky. Once the barley had been distilled, farmers found the resultant discard, known as draff, was a superior feed for livestock. In places like Scotland, devoid of hay, draff was essential for sustaining flocks and herds through winter months. As such, barley became a championed crop.

'UISCE BETHA' IN IRELAND & SCOTLAND

The year 1170 saw a group of English infantrymen sent to dethrone 'Strongbow', the second Earl of Pembroke, who had taken power following his invasion of Ireland. They returned with tales of aqua vitae and *usquebagh*, one of many permutations on the Gaelic *uisce betha*, meaning 'water of life'. When *uisce* is anglicised, we get the word whisky. This spirit, probably infused with herbs and botanicals, could have been distilled from any number of starchy materials.

Though only a potent whisper on English lips, this rumour came six decades before the birth of Ramón Lull. Since inception, distillation knowledge travelled with the movements of scholastic monks. Some left little trace behind save for the unsung propagation of knowledge. These people remain anonymous but they undoubtedly shared spirituous elixirs and the recipes to make them long before the potions encountered people of influence. In 1494 King James IV, a keen medical and scientific enthusiast, bid one Friar Cor make him up a significant amount of aqua vitae. This first appearance of spirit production in an official document, the Scottish Exchequer Rolls, could allude to any number of uses, including to mix with gunpowder. Over the following eighteen years, the Rolls record fifteen more requests for aqua vitae. Undoubtedly, some of this will have been drunk as medicine. So precious was the elixir to James IV, he decided that the making of medicinal *uisce betha* should be solely the remit of the Edinburgh Guild of Barber Surgeons. He granted them a monopoly over production.

PUBLIC DRINKING, TAXATION AND SMUGGLING

But it wasn't long before distillation found its way into the general population. It offered an unparalleled preservation method. The spirits produced in the 1500s right through to the

'Love makes the world go round? Not at all.
Whisky makes it go round twice as fast.'

COMPTON
MACKENZIE

1750s were often made more palatable and 'health-giving' by herbal additions and watered down to a drinkable strength. The popularity of these drinks was soon apparent. In 1556 the Irish government passed a law stating only certain upper-class citizens could distil without a licence. In Scotland by 1579 *uisce betha* became so common that a grain shortage resulted in a ban on production. Only the privileged elite were admitted to continue distilling, but even they were restricted to produce only for their own consumption.

Over the next century or so *uisce betha*'s use as remedy soon evolved into recreation. 1608 saw a license granted in Ireland to Bushmills to begin a significant distilling operation. In Scotland, come 1644, taxation on *uisce betha* was introduced in an attempt to fund the war effort. The 1707 Acts of Union centralised Scottish government in Westminster.

In an attempt to monitor taxation government officials sent excise officers. Eventually distilleries would legally have to provide accommodation for these government agents. Since collection transpired to be uneconomical, with the costs of collecting taxes outweighing income, taxes were raised on spirit production. This led to illicit distilling of bothie (illegal hooch) by many who simply wanted to preserve their grain. Smuggling became a hard but respected way of life – accounts tell of some smugglers who got caught but were released from prison early or allowed to go home on weekends.

Public thirst for whisky only heightened. As an esteemed host, it was your duty to make sure guests got royally intoxicated. If they weren't under the table, you hadn't been hospitable. At funerals in Scotland during the 18th century, it wasn't unheard of that drinking in celebration of the deceased's life would result in others following them to death.

The water of life also came to play an important cultural role as writers and musicians began discovering the pains and pleasures of drinking strong spirit. Following a feast in County Cavan, Irish Gaelic poet Hugh MacGowran wrote *Pléaráca na Ruarcach*. When Jonathan Swift (1667-1745) heard the poem accompanied by the blind harpist Turlough O'Carolan (1670-1738), he asked MacGowran for a literal translation, from which Swift wrote *The Description of an Irish Feast* (1720). In Swift's version, at least one hundred pails of 'usquebagh' are brought to help along festivities, but both poems soon become violent. A little later in the 1700s, Scottish poets such as Robert Burns (1759-1796) and Walter Scott (1771-1832) praised and popularised Scottish whisky far beyond Scotland. In this way, the connotations of the drink spread into the consciousness of people abroad.

NEW INVENTIONS, MORE WHISKIES

Encouraged by new inventions and transportation, such as the steam train, moneyed landowners in the Lowlands began opening legal distilleries or buying those currently operating. Great distilling conglomerates were formed, usually by families. Their aim was to sell both locally and to England for gin production, as whisky could be rectified with botanicals or compounded to make gin. Whereas Highland and Irish whiskey often used 100% malted barley, the Lowlands would use as little as possible to avoid paying excise on the malt tax.

The Highlands had less opportunity to trade with the English. Restricted access meant distillers ran small operations. Often, they were farmers who sold spirit locally. Limited accessibility also meant more illicit stills. The industrious Lowland stills were designed to churn out as much whisky as possible for legal markets. Highland distillers concerned themselves with making the most flavourful whiskies they could. The same was true of Irish stills, which had long been praised. Samuel Johnson exulted the merits of the Irish expression in 1750. Favouritism not only came from the English; Irish whiskey was, in parts of the 19th century, the most imported spirit to America.

One of the most important inventions in the history of distilling was the Coffey still. While two similar stills had been patented previously, Aeneas Coffey's 1830 patent proved technologically superior. The still could run continuously, producing many more times the capacity of even the largest copper-pot stills. Unfortunately, the Irish ex-excise officer had little luck with his countrymen. Though it produced exceptionally pure alcohol, the continuous still also stripped the whiskey of characteristic flavours. Most Irish distillers rejected the still. But it proved to be the perfect tool for the Lowland producers, looking to make as much alcohol as possible.

As early as the 1840s, maturation was notably advertised to denote a superior product. The age statements of whiskies would later become badges of honour. The 1840s also saw the advent of whiskies being blended and promoted with branding. The blending process gave younger whiskies character while older, pungent single malts were tempered by their juvenile counterparts. Blending also offered an opportunity for greater consistency. Even well-made whiskies vary drastically from batch to batch. By the 1880s, improvements in glass manufacture meant more companies began bottling their whiskies as opposed to selling them in barrels. Bottled whisky was easily obtainable and affordable for the masses. It also provided greater control over the product, which until this point could be adulterated in the barrel with all manner of additives by wholesalers or taverns.

DECLINE & REINVENTION

The final decade of the 1800s and first few years of the 1900s brought disaster to both Irish and Scottish distillers. For the Scots it was the conviction of the Pattison brothers – owners of a huge umbrella company covering blenders, exporters and storage facilities. The pair were convicted of fraud and embezzlement. This shattered confidence in what had been a booming market. For the Irish the blow came

from pride in their product. Most producers refused to incorporate the Coffey still into their methods. They simply couldn't complete with the scale of Scottish competition.

The First World War affected both countries. David Lloyd George, British Chancellor of the Exchequer, was heavily in favour of prohibition, fearful that alcohol would have a detrimental effect on production of war supplies. Persuaded in no small part by James Stevens (whose interests were firmly vested with John Walker & Sons) Lloyd George instead facilitated the formation of the Control Board and passed the Immature Spirits Act in 1915. The Control Board was devastating for whiskey producers, reducing public drinking through a series of restrictions, including reducing opening hours, reducing the bottling strength to 40% and even outlawing buying rounds. Paradoxically, this act helped to heighten the quality of whisky by making it a legal requirement that whisky spent at least three years in bond before bottling.

The Irish were further battered by restrictions on alcohol production and barley use in 1917. These measures, coupled with American prohibition beginning in 1920, ruined the Irish market. Were that not bad enough, the Anglo-Irish trade war during the 1930s severed any possible lifeline. Eventually the number of distilleries in Ireland dropped to just two. The Scottish fared better. In fact, prohibition proved prosperous. Huge shipments of blended scotch were exported to America's neighbours: Canada, Mexico and the Caribbean islands. Once there, exporters washed their hands of the whisky's final destination, although special blends were made specifically for American markets. However, just as scotch was beginning to recover from The First World War, The

Second World War caused further problems. A black market for scotch developed as there was a great restriction imposed on the selling of whisky in home markets. The large firms, having set a fixed price, responded admirably. They cut off suppliers they knew to be extortionists and purchased the wildly priced scotch to resell at the fixed price. After the war, government policy on grain allocation and a rise in duties in Britain made a bottle of scotch very expensive. Inadvertently, this was eventually beneficial – scotch still retains its reputation as a luxury product.

With home-grown grain derestricted from ration in 1953 and the free distribution of whisky permitted from 1954, the industry was back on the rise. Scotch experienced another boom in the 60s, but by the 80s and 90s the kids were drinking vodka and rum. Scotch managed to reinvent itself. Single malts, which had generally been used to blend with younger grain whiskies, were championed as excellent in their own right. The distinct and potent flavours of the single malts furthered public opinion that scotch was a drink for the discerning. Thankfully, people's renewed interest in scotch helped the regeneration of the Irish whiskey market, along with sophisticated rebranding efforts from Irish distilleries.

Scotch and Irish whiskies have experienced several peaks and troughs in their lifespans. What endured throughout, in many smaller distilleries, was an uncompromising dedication to the craft. Without this pedigree, neither scotch nor Irish whiskey may have made it into the 21st century with anywhere near the level of high regard they enjoy. Interestingly, none are currently more keen on scotch than the French, who in 2017 bought more in volume of 70cl bottles than any other country.

What is quite staggering is that 2018 saw the Distilled Spirits Council announce Irish whiskey as the fastest growing drinks category. Truly heartening, however, is that the category is no longer being solely dominated by that one Irish blend everyone knows. The once-hailed crafted pot-still whiskey is beginning to make a strong come back.

With distillers increasingly focused on quality, there may never have been a better time to begin enjoying these fine examples of spirits.

'Aye, but today's rain is tomorrow's whisky.'

SCOTTISH
PROVERB

THE BARTENDER'S
CHOICE

SPEED RAIL

Monkey Shoulder Scotch, 40%
Super tasty blend of single malts from
Glenfiddich, Balvenie and Kininvie. This is a
really accessible introduction for someone new
to scotch. Smooth and easy drinking. Mixes
great in cocktails too.

BACK BAR

Connemara Peated Single Malt Whiskey, 40%
Absolute pleasure to drink. Smoky, rich and full,
and for the price it's a steal. If you're into your
Islay whiskies, you'll love this.

TOP SHELF

Highland Park 15 Year Old, 40%

Really special stuff this, from a solid distillery.
I'm a sucker for a sherry cask, which gives this
whisky a lick of sweetness before it dries out.

3 WAYS
TO DRINK
WHISKY

INGREDIENTS

50ml scotch whisky
25ml sweet vermouth
(Fernando de
Castilla Vermut plays
wonderfully)
2-3 dashes of Angostura
bitters

ROB ROY

This scotch brother to its rye counterpart, the Manhattan, was named after Scottish folk hero Rob Roy MacGregor, who Sir Walter Scott glorified in his novel of the same name. The first Rob Roy recipe came out of the original Waldorf Astoria in 1897, before the construction of the Empire State Building necessitated relocation of the famous hotel.

› Add all ingredients to mixing glass / shaker
› Add ice and stir till sufficiently chilled and diluted
› Strain into chilled cocktail coupe
› Garnish with a cherry and enjoy

PENICILLIN

50ml blended scotch
(I've often used Monkey
Shoulder with great
results)
10ml single malt scotch
(Lagavulin 16 if you're
feeling decadent but
Laphroig will do!)
25ml lemon juice
20ml honey water
(1:1 honey:water)
2cm ginger disk
(skin removed)

Bartender Sam Ross made this instant classic whilst working at Milk and Honey in New York. Never fails to wow. The original calls for the peaty scotch to be floated on top, although I like the smokiness mixed, curling around the other flavours. Why not try both?

› Muddle ginger in shaking tin

› Add the remaining ingredients

› Shake furiously for 12-15 seconds

› Double strain into a rocks glass

› Add ice (best not use a straw if you've floated the whisky)

› Garnish with candied ginger or a slice of ginger

CHECK MATE

Really tasty after-dinner beverage that I created on St. Paddy's day. The ingredients are a bit of an investment for a home bar, but if you're well stocked, this is delicious. If not, ask your favourite bartender to fix one up for you.

› Begin by rinsing cocktail coupe with Chartreuse
› Add remaining ingredients to mixing glass / shaker
› Add ice and stir till sufficiently chilled and diluted
› Discard Chartreuse and strain into cocktail coupe

'The light music of whiskey falling into a glass
— an agreeable interlude.'

JAMES
JOYCE

CURIOSITIES

Following his father's death five years earlier, Tommy Dewar joined the family business, John Dewar and Sons, alongside his brother John Alexander (J.A.). The spirited entrepreneur's first act was to take himself off to London to drum up business. He secured a stand at the Brewers Exhibition. But being the only scotch promoter at the show wasn't enough for Tommy. To draw attention to his wares he paid a piper in a kilt to parade by the stall playing bagpipes – much to the horror of the other exhibitors. Though many pleaded with Tommy to stop the din, Tommy kept the piper playing, securing some lucrative contracts in the process.

The word *sláinte* is a Gaelic toast to health. It is only used when spirits are being drunk, reminiscent of times when spirits were seen as medicinal.

The Scots didn't always champion their own stock. Irish whiskey during the 1860s held the accolade of being the most sold type of whisky in Scotland.

SHŌCHŪ
焼酎

Since 2003 shōchū has been more popular in Japan than saké, yet most people outside of Japan have no idea what shōchū is. The story of this less potent spirit is counter to that of nearly every other. Whereas most drinks developed through constant collaboration and influence from other countries, shōchū was largely a product of isolation. This makes it, along with baijiu, one of the most distinctive drinks in the world. It is also one of the most varied in its use of ingredients. The Japanese attention to detail produced a fine spirit, which is beginning to garner praise globally.

WHAT IS SHŌCHŪ?

Pronounced 'show chew', shōchū is a traditional Japanese spirit distilled from the ferment of a wide variety of vegetables, grain, and sugar. The most common ingredients used to make shōchū are sweet potato, rice, barley, buckwheat (soba) and brown sugar. The fermentation of these ingredients in shōchū production requires a substance known as kōji. Kōji is a steamed starchy block, often made of rice, barley, sweet potato or buckwheat, which is inoculated with a specific family of fungus called *Aspergillus*. Rice kōji is commonly used in saké production and the family of moulds are also used to make soy sauce and bean pastes. There are three different types

of kōji – white, black and yellow – whose different cultures produce different flavours when combined with the ingredients they ferment.

After the kōji has been made, it is married with water and yeast to begin fermentation. Once fermentation has started, the kōji is introduced to the ingredient producers wish to ferment. Since two different fermentation processes take place, shōchū is twice fermented. Following fermentation, the ingredients are distilled to produce spirit. During fermentation and distillation, all ingredients remain in a solid or semi-solid state.

There are two different types of shōchū – otsu-rui (often referred to as 'honkaku' or 'authentic' shōchū) and ko-rui. Otsu-rui is only distilled once in a pot still and has strict parameters around what, where and how it is made. Ko-rui is a rectified shōchū, meaning it is distilled more than once, often in a column still. Once distilled, shōchū can be aged in wooden barrels, earthenware pots or stainless steel vats. Aged shōchū is known as koshu and it is usually aged between one and three years. After ageing, some producers choose to filter the spirit before dilution.

Shōchū is often bottled at a lower strength than other spirits at around 25-30% but some reach strengths of 35-40%. Shōchū is made all over Japan, although the main areas of production are Kyūshū Island and Okinawa Prefecture. Four distinctive shōchūs are protected by the World Trade Organisation in the same way spirits such as cognac are protected by an Appellation d'Origine Contrôlée. These four styles are called Iki, Kuma, Ryūkyū and Satsuma. Shōchū is drunk neat, with ice, with hot or cold water (usually at a ratio of 6:4 water: shōchū) and in cocktails.

RICE & TUBERS

Rice is the seed of a member of the grass family. The crop may have been cultivated for 7-10,000 years, with the earliest written records emerging from China around 2800 BCE. There are over 40,000 varieties of rice, which fall into two main species. The rice species *Oryza sativa* originated in Asia and may be indigenous to China, India and Thailand. African rice, *Oryza glaberrima*, was first cultivated around the Niger River delta. It is possible that wetland farming of rice was introduced to certain Japanese islands such as Kyūshū up to 3,000 years ago – however, this didn't become widespread until the Yayoi Period (300 BCE-250 CE). Wetland farming found its way to Japan through trade with China, Korea and Thailand, the latter of which still provides a large proportion of rice used in the production of shōchū.

Rice enjoys a rich cultural history, being the subject of much myth and folklore. Its association with fertility still carries with it the tradition of throwing rice at weddings.

Sweet potatoes, tubers of a perennial vine, are indigenous to Chile and Peru. These vegetables have been cultivated by native civilisations for up to 4,500 years. They were one of the spoils Columbus brought back with him in the 1490s. They were commonly known as potatoes until the similar looking, less sweet spud made its way into European cultures in the 1740s. Sweet potatoes were believed to be an aphrodisiac. These hardy nutritious storage organs have the ability to grow in poor soil conditions. In Kyūshū, where the volcanic soil cannot sustain rice or other crops, the sweet potato became a lifeline for farmers. It would also become a choice ingredient in making shōchū.

EARLY DRINKING – VIRGINS AND SERPENTS

The ancient history of Japanese drinking is far less traceable than that of other cultures. Oceanic isolation denied the Japanese development of the written word. As such the first record of intoxication in Japan comes from the Chinese. In the year 297 CE, *The History of the Kingdom of Wei* reports that the Japanese had affection for drinking. But it's difficult to know exactly how long indigenous people had been drinking for. The first written evidence of interaction with the Chinese comes in the first decade of the Common Era. This might suggest the beginnings of a relationship, including alcoholic trade and technology. That said, ancient Japanese pottery reveals the use of fruit to make alcohol dating from the Jomon period (12,000-300 BCE). What is for certain is that when the ancient Japanese did discover drinking, they developed a great affinity for it.

In Japan, any type of alcohol was and still is referred to as saké. The 'rice wine' known as saké in the West is actually called nihonshu and is made in a closer manner to beer than wine. Once the Japanese began documenting their inebriated antics they created rich tales worth telling over a drink. The Nara Period (710-794 CE) offered the first opportunity for these to be documented by Japanese hands. The first two texts recording the history and folklore of Japan by the Japanese are the *Kojiki* (712 CE) and the *Nihon Shoki* or *Nihongi* (720 CE). Both these texts present a version of a story in which the Shinto god of storms and sea, Susanoo-no-Mikoto, kills an eight-headed serpent after getting the monster so drunk it passed out. In the *Nihongi*, Susanoo encounters an elderly couple, also gods, distraught about the approaching birth of the child they'd conceived. Susanoo learned that the couple had

'Today, gloriously drunk, we no longer know the meaning of unhappiness.'

RYŌKAN
TAIGU

seven children previously. The eight-headed serpent had taken every child at birth. Susanoo bade the couple to brew enough saké (alcohol) from as many fruits as they could find to fill eight jars. When the child was born, the serpent arrived in timely fashion. Susanoo, in the guise of an offering, bade each head drink one of the jars. When the sloshed serpent fell into a drunken slumber, Susanoo hacked it to death, breaking his sword in the process. Fortuitously he found a new, better sword inside the slain snake.

Around this time, in the *Harima no Kuni Fudoki*, (725 CE) (Geography and Culture of Harima Province) came the first mention of kōji. This magic starter block, probably in use some years earlier, was adopted from Chinese qu. It revolutionised the production of alcoholic drinks. Prior to the arrival of kōji, *kuchikamizake* was often the way to turn rice into alcohol. *Kuchikamizake* means 'mouth-chewed alcohol'. Since the starch in rice needs to be converted into sugars to be fermentable, and rice can't be malted, the amylase enzyme in saliva was used to convert the starch to sugars. The ferment was generally drunk with rice grains still present, like a boozy porridge. Interestingly enough, in elite circles, the job of rice chewing was designated to young unmarried maidens. The resultant virginal brew was known as *bijinshu*, or 'beautiful woman's saké'.

Even with the appearance of kōji, the Japanese had another seven hundred years to wait until the technology for turning fermented rice into spirit arrived.

ISLANDS OF DISTILLATION, GRAFFITI & THE SWEET POTATO

The initial references to distillation are scattered across

the Japanese islands and no doubt developed separately from several different influences. The first comes from the Kingdom of Ryūkyū (modern Okinawa) in 1477, which remained under independent imperial rule until 1879. Since Ryūkyū had been in trade with the Siamese (now Thailand), they had developed a taste for spirits and decided to distil their own. By around 1515, Ryūkyūan merchants were clocked searching for the most potent drinks they could find in Malaysian markets by Portuguese explorer Tomé Pires. The merchants left with lots of spirit, which Tomé thought similar to brandy. Apparently, the Portuguese were rather interested in Japanese activity in the 16th century. Come 1546, Jorges Ávarez's travels took him to Yamagawa on the isle of Kyūshū. There he reported the Japanese drinking rice arrack. Arrack, a word with permutations from Java to Mongolia, always translates as a distilled spirit. But the first known mention of the word shōchū, meaning 'burnt alcohol', comes from the most unlikely of places.

1559 saw the construction of the Kōriyama Hachiman shrine, overseen by a high priest. Two disgruntled labourers working on the site became fed up with their employer. In an attempt to vent their frustrations, they decided to indulge in a spot of vandalism on the sacred structure. They carved their grievances into one of the rafters. The lines complained the priest was a cheapskate, since he'd not once given them any shōchū, and exclaimed what a nuisance this was. These bold pre-unionists even signed and dated their act of protest. It would be wrong not to give them a mention. Their names were Sakujirō and Suketarō Tsuruta.

Since our two friends felt so wronged by the high priest's

tight-fistedness, it follows that shōchū, at least in parts of Kyūshū, may have been used as currency. It also gives the impression that shōchū wasn't completely new or out of the reach of the peasant class at this point in time.

By great luck, in the first decade of the 17th century the sweet potato found its way to Ryūkyū in the care of Noguni Sōkan. Before the Japanese closed themselves off to the world the sweet potato found itself behind the isolating wall. In 1705 a fisherman by the name of Riemon Maeda returned to Yamagawa from a trip to Ryūkyū bearing the tubers, which he proceeded to plant and trade with local farmers. The year 1732 saw grain crops fail. 12,000 dead was the catastrophic outcome. The sweet potato weathered the failure and the hundreds who had adopted the crop were spared. Maeda became a hero and Kyūshū acquired

a new and deeply significant crop to distil with. It would eventually overtake rice as the most commonly used organic material in shōchū production for this area.

THE CLOSING AND OPENING OF JAPAN

Japan had a relatively peaceful time during the Tokugawa Shogunate, also known as the Edo period (1603-1868). This was when a samurai government had administrative rule of Japan from Edo (modern day Tokyo). The Emperor, who resided in Kyoto, was merely symbolically appointed during this period. Japan implemented a foreign policy of sakoku, completely locking down trade and travel into and out of Japan. The only exceptions were strict trades conducted with the Dutch and the Chinese. This meant, like in Japan's distant past, very little outside influence penetrated the country. For shōchū production, this halted any kind of great progress for more than 250 years – however, this wasn't necessarily a bad thing. Honkaku shōchū is still single distilled, a rarity among distillates. Producers retained many traditional techniques, which is what makes shōchū such a unique spirit.

It is unfortunate that not much shōchū was drunk by the peasant class at this time. Throughout the Edo period the samurai, highest in the hierarchical feudal system, tended to restrict drinking to festival days. In Ryūkyū during the 18th and 19th centuries, if peasants were caught distilling illegally, the penalty was death.

Thankfully for the thirsty peasants, an American commodore named Matthew Perry was about to disrupt over two centuries of peace and apply great pressure to open Japan. In 1853 Perry arrived at the port of Edo with two sailboats and two steam-powered boats. He took examples of advanced technology to impress and intimidate the Japanese. Thus displayed, he delivered an ultimatum of trade or aggression. The Shōgun was put in an impossible position and had to acquiesce to the power of the United States. The Shōgun's perceived betrayal of Japan led the Emperor to rally a band of imperialists to rebel. The Emperor seized power by 1868, marking the beginning of the Meiji period, which would last until 1912. Japan and shōchū production were once again open to the influences of the world.

NEW TECHNOLOGY – STILLS & THE ATOMIC BOMB

By 1895 Aeneas Coffey's still had found its way to Japan. This meant shōchū could be made cheaper than before and on a much larger scale. Despite potential financial gains, many rejected this new technology. As ever though, opportunists did adopt the still and 1910 saw the advent of a new kind of shōchū. This double-distilled version, made in the more economic column still, became known as kō-rui. Rather than choosing one style of shōchū over the other, people took to mixing the two types of spirit together, creating a homemade blend. For the consumption of shōchū itself, this was a good thing. For the first time cheap and strong booze could be drunk by labourers. They embraced shōchū over saké in the regions where shōchū was made, since it packed more of a punch relative to price. Saké was still very much associated with the moneyed classes, meaning it garnered international acclaim sooner, but kō-rui shōchū's price and strength put it in the hands of the people.

Along with new tax laws on production, this affected many traditional producers. It spurred those who made the single-distilled variety of shōchū, otsu-rui, to work on improving their methods. This helped prompt the discovery of kōji kin in 1920, the specific white fungus used widely in both shōchū and saké production.

The trauma of the Second World War would only make it harder for makers of otsu-rui to establish stable trade. Following 1945, people decimated emotionally and financially by war would drown their sorrows in black market alcohol. This phenomenon was termed 'kasutori culture'. Kasutori was a specific type of shōchū, distilled from the lees of saké production. However, the culture had little to do with what was and is a fine example of shōchū. Post-war spirits sold on the black market were often adulterated with countless impurities and poisons. A particularly vile mix of methanol (toxic to humans), cut with chemicals to mask flavour was dubbed 'bakudan', the bomb, reflecting the self-destructive nature of kasutori culture.

Without the death penalty looming over would-be distillers and with demand for illicit booze high, clandestine production exploded. In the 1950s it wasn't unusual for 40,000 people a year to be arrested for distilling without permission. This made many consumers turn to imported spirits, which they knew would be less likely to harm them.

THE SHŌCHŪ RENAISSANCE & INTERNATIONAL MARKETS

Thankfully, by 1976 the first of three shōchū booms began. Associations with kasutori culture had dwindled and the ritual of mixing hot water with spirit at a ratio of 6:4 became popular. For the first time, consumers were beginning to see the merits of otsu-rui, the single-distilled predecessor to kō-rui. Shōchū, along with its Okinawan cousin, awamori, eventually received enough praise to condone a yearly celebration, first held November, 1987.

Since 2003 shōchū has become more popular than saké in Japan and has enjoyed a stable position amongst other alcoholic drinks. 2014 saw shōchū given its own spirits category by the IWSC (International Wine & Spirits Competition). With increasing use in global bars and interest from spirits enthusiasts around the globe, shōchū may be about to experience a boom in demand like never before. Such versatility in how shōchū is drunk and its natural affinity with food pairing, thanks to its many, styles, flavours and strengths, mean it is gaining international favour with the adventurous. Given time, this little-known marvel of the past may just become the drink of the future.

THE BARTENDER'S CHOICE

SPEED RAIL

Takara Towari Honkaku, 25%
I slightly hesitate at recommending this as a first try, but if you're going to have a crack at shōchū, you're probably adventurous. Have a go with some spiced food or meats. I get smoke from this, like a very delicate Islay whisky, along with something savoury like cheese. Sounds strange but you can't help sucking your tongue after you've drunk it.

BACK BAR

Satoh, 25%

I could spend an afternoon with this on a hot day. Made with handpicked sweet potato and black koji, this honkaku shōchū is deep and rich but also has a delicateness about it. It has something close to black sesame in the flavour.

TOP SHELF

Toyonaga Okokuma, 40%

I've found a new favourite in this rice shōchū, aged for seven years in sherry casks. It's like an amarone grappa laced with oloroso sherry. I really can't speak more highly of its caramel, toffee, prune and fig flavours. What adds to the pleasure of drinking this is knowing only 400 bottles are released a year!

3WAYS
TODRINK
SHŌCHŪ

LOW-PROOF HI-BALL

INGREDIENTS

75ml yuzu shōchū
125ml soda water

I think this is a great twist on the classic Japanese hi-ball, and the yuzu adds another layer of refreshment.

› Place shōchū in a Collins glass
› Fill to very top with ice
› Pour in soda slowly and stir twice
› Express lemon twist over drink
  and discard

KIMONO SILK

INGREDIENTS

50ml plum (ume) shōchū
25ml London dry gin
1 dash lemon bitters

Really delicate and refreshing. A nice way to introduce someone to a martini-style drink if they're not acquainted.

› Begin chilling cocktail coupe
› Place all ingredients into a mixing glass
› Add ice and stir until sufficiently diluted
› Discard ice in coupe and strain drink
  into glass

REMAIN SOBA

INGREDIENTS

50ml buckwheat
(soba) shōchū
25ml sweet vermouth
2 dashes Angostura
bitters

This is a low-alcohol version of the Manhattan with a lighter, more delicate flavour. Don't be fooled by the name – it will still get you drunk!

› Begin chilling cocktail coupe
› Place all ingredients into a mixing glass
› Add ice and stir until sufficiently diluted
› Discard ice in coupe and strain drink into glass

'Even in the time of the gods
They needed wine
To deceive others."

KARAI
SENRYŪ

CURIOSITIES

Shōchū can be made out of a staggering range of different organic materials, over 50. They include aloe, cactus, carrot, devil's tongue, gingko nuts, kelp, radish, sesame and tomatoes. The distinction in category and flavour from other spirits comes in the production process rather than the actual ingredients.

Japan's third largest island, Kyūshū, produces a large proportion of the shōchū made in the country. The island inhabitants also hold claim to consuming almost double the amount of shōchū compared to their fellow citizens.

By the early 1900s shōchū was a huge part of daily life in southern Kyūshū Japan. An American academic, Ella Wiswell, tells of being served shōchū in the 1930s, both at a baby naming party and a child vaccination at a school!

TEQUILA & MEZCAL

Never is tequila uttered without some acknowledgement the night will be eventful. The word seems to act as an incantation for partying and frivolity. From its sacred status among Mesoamerican cultures, the agave plant became an indispensable asset in the Mexican economy, with tequila as its star progeny. But tequila and mezcal could also be seen as a symbol for the tension between industrial expansion and artisanal heritage. Tireless modernisation and promotion left a golden hue in pockets and across culture. Artists, holidaymakers and barflies remain insatiable for a drink which embodies sunshine. But such accelerated growth led to a historical hangover. Even today, producers, the tequileros and mezcaleros, wildlife and the agave plants face problems. Tequila, deeply rooted in Mexican history, regionally specific and made from a plant of great importance to cultural identity, holds a unique place among the world's spirits.

WHAT IS TEQUILA?

Tequila can only be made from a certain type of agave plant, *Agave tequilana*, known as blue agave or Weber's Azul. These agaves have a bluish hue to their green leaves. Their bulbs are known as hearts, heads or piñas, because of their resemblance to a pineapple once the leaves have been removed. Unlike with mezcal, where the hearts are traditionally baked in huge pits in the earth, many

tequileros cook the hearts in autoclaves. This makes the flavour profile of tequilas less smoky than mezcals.

The cooking process allows the naturally occurring molecule inulin to be converted to fructose. This is used as the sugar for fermentation. After the hearts have been cooked they are milled to release sugary juice, which is fermented and then distilled. Tequila has to be made of at least 51% Weber's Azul but many producers choose to make it from 100% blue agave. If other sugars, such as cane juice, are added prior to fermentation the tequila is known as a mixto. Tequila is generally made in the Mexican state of Jalisco, although Mexican law dictates tequila can also be made in the states of Guanajuato, Michoacán, Nayarit and Tamaulipas.

There are five types of tequila. *Blanco* tequila, also known as silver, plata, white or platinum tequila, can be bottled right after distillation or stored in stainless steel vats for up to two months. Reposado (rested) is aged in barrels between two months and a year. Joven or gold tequila can be a blend of aged and unaged tequila but frequently (and unfortunately) tends to be a mixto with added colourants, such as caramel, and flavourings. Añejo (aged) tequila is barrel aged from one year up to three years. A new category of tequila emerged in 2006 known as extra añejo (extra old). These are any tequilas aged over three years. Some are aged up to 10 years with the oldest tequilas in the world being over 20 years old.

WHAT IS MEZCAL?

The three main differences between mezcal and tequila are locale, species and the aforementioned production methods. Mezcal must be made in one of nine states, with the majority of mezcals produced in Oaxaca – the other eight states are Durango, Guanajuato, Guerrero, Michoacán, San Luis Potosí, Tamaulipas, Puebla and Zacatecas, some of which overlap with tequila regions. Unlike tequila, mezcal can be made with many types of agave and around 30 varieties are used for production. The most common of these is espadín, but each variety offers nuance in flavour and different agaves may be blended together to give unique results. Mezcal also comes in classifications of *blanco, reposado* and *añejo*.

A SACRED HEART

More than 200 known species of the agave plant, or maguey, exist across the landmass spanning from Southern Canada to Peru. This family of succulents are sometimes mistaken for cactus or aloe vera because of the sharp spikes running along the edge of their leaves. As well as a food source, early civilisations used agave for shelter, making roofing of the great leaves. The fibrous leaf strands provided thread for cloth and even the thorns of the plant could be utilised as needles. Agave nectar, still a popular sweetener, was another heralded yield from the plant. These perennials, often cooked in roasting pits, could have been harvested for up to 12,000 years by Mesoamerican cultures.

Ancient myth reveals that magueys were seen as sacred beings by indigenous peoples. Mayans held shamanic rituals with pulque – a milky alcoholic drink of about 4-8%. This was made by extracting and fermenting the sweet sap (aguamiel), of one of five or so different species of agave. The Aztecs gave maguey a goddess, Mayahuel, the goddess of fertility. Her husband, Patecatl, was accredited with the discovery of fermentation. Both he and his wife were the gods of pulque. It's with little surprise that the couple, bestowed with stewardship of the inebriating pulque, together parented four hundred rabbits – the Centzon Totochtin. Collectively these rabbits were the gods of drunkenness.

Being honoured as a holy intoxicant didn't stop there. When naming the plant genus in 1753, the patriarch of modern taxonomy, Carl Linnaeus, chose a name meaning noble or desirable. In doing so he also invoked the Greek goddess, Agave. As one of the Maenads, or 'raving ones', Agave was one of the female disciples of Dionysus, the god of all things wine. As serious as he was about the categorisation of living organisms, it seems the Swedish naturalist wasn't without a sense of humour. Agave is also known in English as the century plant. While this may be an exaggeration of the plant's average 25 to 40-year lifespan, some specimens have been known to live up to 50 years. With such an illustrious family history, it is easy to see how one species of agave went on to produce a drink as iconic as tequila, with its lesser-known sister mezcal being no less revered by connoisseurs.

REALITY REFLECTS MYTH – THE UNCLEAR HISTORY OF DISTILLATION

It is a saddening irony that the creation of tequila began with the demise of the Aztecs. Strangely prophetic, several versions of Aztec creationist myths on agave speak of Mayahuel's murder, her body and bones transformed into the sacred plant. In 1519,

'Sublime is something you choke on
after a shot of tequila.'

MARK Z.
DANIELEWSKI

Hernán Cortés landed along the Yucatan coast of Mexico, intent on conquering in the name of the Spanish crown. On reaching the Aztec capital Tenochtitlán he was greeted by a welcoming party sent by emperor Moctezuma. Cortés' arrival aligned with a prophecy marking the return of the Aztec god, Quetzalcoatl. Moctezuma believed this may have been who was approaching his kingdom. Cortés, unaware of this, stormed a city which was expecting to greet a god. Moctezuma was captured and used to puppet Cortés' rule. The Aztecs rebelled and Cortés fled, but one of his men lay dead in the great city, killed in battle whilst carrying smallpox.

Infection spread among the Aztecs. With no immunity, the population was decimated by the disease. Some three million Aztecs lost their lives to the epidemic. Weakened in numbers and strength, the city once more succumbed to Spanish rule. But disease and death were not all the conquistadors brought with them. While pulque may have been consumed for well over 2,000 years, one key element was missing to transform the ferment of agave into spirit: distillation.

Intriguing evidence suggests the potential for distillation by indigenous Mesoamericans long before the arrival of Cortés. Crude, still-like pots and miniature cups, pointless for pulque, have been found. Others theorise that Filipinos arrived with distillation technology resembling early Chinese efforts – hollowed tree trunks – in the mid-1500s. Whether or not pre-Columbian distillation did exist, the Spanish invasion led to an influx of distillation methods and materials. A distillate by the name of *vino de mezcal* began to emerge. This was often produced for medicinal purposes, reminiscent of the herbal tinctures of Europe. Inevitably, people began drinking their distilled agave spirits recreationally. These were initially made in meagre proportions by farming families – but as ever with the production of spirits, there was never quite enough.

CULTIVARS & A LITTLE TOWN CALLED TEQUILA

While agaves had already been clone-cultivated well before the Spanish conquering, the demand for vino de mezcal in the mid-18th century vastly accelerated the process of cultivation. Agaves have the ability to propagate in two ways. Sexually, they are monocarpic, giving the plants only one chance to spread their seed. Once they reach maturity, a long staff, known as a quiote, grows from their bulbs high into the air. The tips of the quiotes flower. In a similar way to bee pollination, nectar-feeding bats oblige in the reproduction process. Agaves can also reproduce asexually by creating clones of themselves. This ability to reproduce identical replicas presented a unique opportunity for farming. During the time which agaves began to be cultivated for production of vino de mezcal, several species were singled out for superior qualities. Choice features included: relatively quick maturation; a disposition to local conditions and altitudes (since different agave plants favour different conditions); and finer-tasting hearts once roasted and distilled. Some plants gave sweet juices, others bitter and astringent. Among numerous agaves cultivated in this way was the blue agave, later named Weber's Azul.

José Antonio de Cuervo secured the first land grant

from the King of Spain to grow agaves and distil *vino de mezcal* in 1758. Cuervo chose a town where Franciscan monks had made their home over 200 years earlier, on the east side of a dormant volcano. The town was called Tequila, meaning 'place of work'. The rich volcanic soil was mineral-charged by an eruption some 220,000 years prior. This, coupled with ambient conditions in altitude and rainfall, offered a perfect home for many of the agave species used to make *vino de mezcal*. Cuevo's distillery was the first to legally produce *vino de mezcal*, providing revenue in taxes for the Spanish crown. Optimum conditions meant the agave flourished and the 1820 Mexican war of Independence contributed twofold to the popularity of mezcal. Soldiers loved the drink. And once Mexico won the war, importing Spanish spirits was understandably

difficult. Mezcal slowly trickled into the hearts of locals.

The 1870s saw an employee of the Cuevo distillery, Cenobio Sauza, take his skills and start his own distillery and brand. Tequila, shrewdly marketed as Mexican whisky for an American market, began to make its way north of the border. Both companies attest to being the first to sell tequila commercially to the United States. In 1875 the area's reputation for fine mezcal preceded itself – mezcal from the region became known as *mezcal de Tequila*. An astute entrepreneur, Sauza went a step further, securing a place at the 1893 World Columbia Exhibition. His contributions did very well. Abroad, his award winning *mezcal de Tequila* made the terroir synonymous with quality and craftsmanship.

By the time America's great prohibition experiment began

in 1920, tequila, as it had become known, was already on the lips of many Americans. Taxes on spirits made tequila a prosperous commodity for the Mexican government. This was reflected in its numerous efforts to protect the spirit's name by creating parameters around how was made. This included the adoption of blue agave as the true heart of tequila, later made law by a Denominación de Origen (DO). These stipulations were driven by the tequila companies seeking to benefit from a more distinctive product. The companies reinvested in modern equipment, endeavouring to make tequila production as economically streamlined as possible. Earthen pits became clay ovens; these were eventually replaced with autoclaves. Likewise, mills traditionally made of volcanic stone and powered by donkey were done away with. Only two remaining aspects could not be replicated by machines – the year-round attentiveness farmers gave the agave and the skill of the jimadores. The jimadores still work in blistering heat to harvest the weighty piñas, cutting precisely, with generational knowledge of what to remove, from where, and at what stage of the agaves' development.

WELCOME TO MARGARITAVILLE

Tequila was an exotic easy sell from bootleggers to the booze-deprived US. Adventurous tourists drunk tequila readily in the romance of sunshine. Cocktail culture helped bolster this with delicious drinks like the margarita being shaken up. *On The Road* author Jack Kerouac famously loved the drink and is often quoted, 'Don't drink to get drunk. Drink to enjoy life.' Sadly, he may have enjoyed life a little too much, dying of liver complications at 47. Musicians too took inspiration from the spirit. Covered by the Ventures, The Champs' 1958 'Tequila' went from being a B-side record to a #1 hit.

For Mexicans themselves, tequila lost its appeal as French products became the *bois de jour*. In an attempt to renew thirst, tequila companies used product placement in the mid-1900s. Charros, the Mexican answer to cowboys, were featured drinking tequila in films. This served to embed tequila in Mexican identity. Meanwhile, the West began a masochistic love affair with tequila. It became the drink to get drunk on. Frozen margaritas and shots led to forgetful mornings and hazy regret, epitomised in Terrorvision's 1998 hit, 'Tequila'. The salt and lime ritual developed to distract taste buds from badly-made mixtos. The shooting culture was brilliant for the profits of the big tequila companies, but terrible for smaller artisan producers, as well as tequila's poor sister mezcal.

But the meteoric success story of tequila came with consequences. The narrow gene pool of blue agave plants, the result of persistent cloning, left them vulnerable. Blue agave suffered from gangrenous diseases, bacterial infection and agave-eating snout weevils. This echoed the disaster of phylloxera on the vineyards of Europe, which undoubtedly helped tequila reach a wider audience. It wasn't just agaves that were affected by industrialisation. Two species of long-nosed bat, which aid the propagation of agave, increasingly lost access to their food source. The practice of jimadores cutting quiotes before they flowered to preserve flavourful nutrients left the bats little to feed on. And finally, although some efforts were made to protect farmers, huge companies monopolised the market, giving them the power to dictate agave prices. The agave cultivators frequently got raw deals on their produce. Even today these problems haven't been eradicated.

Thankfully for everyone, attitudes and markets are changing. Bar luminaries have looked at tequila through the lens of research and strived to cultivate a more educated clientele for the drink. Dedicated scientists such as Ana Valenzuela-Zapata and Gary Nabhan work tirelessly with tequileros and mezcaleros in an attempt to conserve the delicate balance between plant and industry, addressing potentially damaging practices.

Popular culture is as demanding as ever. Tequila is the drink of choice for many rappers, who champion certain brands of tequila as their predecessors did with cognac in the 90s and 00s.

But even here, there seems a shift in favoured brands towards more refined products. The renewed appreciation for what tequila can be at its best is heartening. A drink with its roots planted in the divine is slowly becoming treasured once more. Rather than being recklessly necked, it is sipped, savoured and gratefully appreciated.

THE BARTENDER'S
CHOICE

SPEED RAIL

Aquariva Reposado, 38%

This is actress Cleo Rocos' answer to an affordable 100% blue agave premium tequila. The agave notes stand up to mixing, while the oak resting gives smoothness and subtlety. It's decent fare for sipping or mixing. A speed rail favourite.

BACK BAR

Tapatio Blanco, 40%

When Carlos Camarena, a hero of distilling in the tequila world, decides to make his own tequila, you know it's going to shine. Worth sipping neat, this is a great expression of just how wonderful blanco tequila can be.

TOP SHELF

Fortaleza Añejo, 40%

Guillermo Sauza, once heir to the Sauza tequila distillery, returned to traditional craftsmanship with complete disregard for industrial processes. Production methods are skilled, laborious and artisanal – a *tahona* (traditional mill) is used to mill agave heads. This, coupled with an unparalleled drive for quality, makes for an impeccable tequilaria. Expect the brown buttery sweetness of caramel, toffee and butterscotch with hints of spice and citrus. A gift from the gods.

3 WAYS
TO DRINK
TEQUILA
& MEZCAL

MARGARITA

50ml blanco/ reposado
tequila
20ml Cointreau
25ml lime juice

You might be forgiven for thinking a drink in the daisy family of cocktails wouldn't be much of a heavy hitter with writers, bartenders and boozehounds. Dangerously drinkable, this classic served sans-ice, with a little foam cap from vigorous elbow grease, is a joy to drink. To salt the rim of your glass, use a lime wedge to paint a wet stripe along it, then roll in some finely crushed sea salt.

› Add all ingredients to cocktail shaker
› Shake as hard as possible for 12-15 seconds
› Double strain into a chilled cocktail coupe

PALOMA

50ml tequila
30ml pink grapefruit juice
15ml lime juice
5ml sugar syrup
Soda top

There are few things more refreshing than a Paloma. If you know of any, do tell.

› Add all ingredients to Collins glass / hi-ball (except soda)
› Fill glass to very top with ice
› Top with soda and stir gently
› Garnish with grapefruit wheel or wedge

MEXIQUITO NEGRONI

Vegetal, creamy and bittersweet – a great alternative for those who haven't quite developed a taste for the bitter negroni.

25ml reposado tequila
25ml Cynar
25ml sweet vermouth
(Cocchi Vermouth di
Torino makes a fine
drink)
2 dashes orange bitters

› Add all ingredients to a mixing glass
› Fill with ice and stir to taste
› Strain into rocks glass
› Fill with fresh ice
› Express oils of orange twist and garnish drink with peel

'We should all believe in something, and I
believe it's time for another shot of tequila.'

JUSTIN
TIMBERLAKE

'One tequila, two tequila, three tequila, floor.'

GEORGE
CARLIN

C U R I O S I T I E S

Tequila should never come with a worm. The worm, which does appear in some mezcal bottles, is the larva of a moth. Some mezcal marketers thought it was a good idea to include one in the bottle as a sales gimmick.

There are other mezcals in Mexico that have regionally specific names and are made from specific agave plants. The most common of these are bacanora and raicilla.

Scientists at the Autonomous University of Mexico have found a way to synthesise diamonds from tequila. Whilst the diamonds are too small to make jewellery, they can be sharpened to make medical tools or used to replace silicon components in circuitry.

BOURBON

The roots of bourbon and rye are in many ways grafts of Irish and Scottish culture onto a new continent. The discovery of maize by settlers offered a never-before distilled crop, which would produce a distinctly regional spirit. The story of American whiskies, from the offset, is one of rebellion. What has emerged from four hundred years of volatile resistance is a drink worthy of its place among the other spirits of the world. Like all spirits these whiskies have a dubious past. But they also acted as catalyst for progression. It is a shame that these whiskies, often looked upon as inferior to their Scotch and Irish counterparts, rarely receive the praise they deserve outside of their devoted followers.

WHAT IS BOURBON?

Bourbon is a barrel-aged spirit distilled from fermented corn and other cereals, including malted barley, wheat and rye. The mash bill of grains must contain at least 51% corn. The distillate can reach a maximum strength of 80% ABV. Once distilled the produced spirit, known as 'white dog', must go into unused charred American white oak barrels. No other barrel will do. The whiskey can only enter the barrel at a maximum of 62.5% ABV. Once it's in the barrel, interestingly, there is no minimum age required for bourbon itself; however, its subcategories do impose time restraints.

Nowhere along the line may any additives be used in bourbon. And, finally, bourbon must be bottled at no less than 40% ABV.

If producers would like to call their product straight bourbon, it must be aged for at least two years. If they would like to do this and not have to put an age statement on the bottle, they must age it for more than four years. Single barrel bourbon, unsurprisingly, comes from just one barrel of whiskey. With small-batch bourbon, it becomes slightly trickier as there are no real outlines as to what defines a small batch. The whiskey in the bottle is a blend from a batch of barrels but the number of barrels is completely up to the discretion of the producer. This isn't intrinsically indicative of quality but suggests some poor chap had to taste lots of bourbon and decide which would best marry up. There are also blends, which must contain at least 51% corn, but may have additives or colourings added. One little question may be niggling. Bourbon isn't specifically from Kentucky, although around 95% of the world's bourbon is made there.

A NEW WORLD CROP & OLD WORLD SUSPICIONS

Maize, or corn, is a cereal crop, which has been cultivated for over 6,000 years by Native Americans. It is thought Mesoamericans originally domesticated the grain in modern Mexico, around 7,000 years ago. Maize's unparalleled agricultural significance spread north and south. The crop offered a staple food supply to support pre-colonial cities such as Cahokia. Founded around 600 CE, by the mid-1200s this Mississippian city housed some 15,000 Native Americans, a population of a similar size to London at that time. Indigenous peoples of the Americas found that maize, along with everything from maple sap to maguey, was fermentable. Both Mesoamerican and Native American cultures frequently brewed maize, although it was often imbibed under great restrictions, reserved for religious ceremonies.

The first decade of the 1600s saw the first influx of pilgrim and Puritan settlers to North America. Many sought to practice their religious beliefs free from persecution. The majority settled on the eastern seaboard in what would become the fledgling states. As the population grew, it pushed further inland across the western frontier. Some of the first English, Irish and Scottish immigrants to America were suspicious of 'Indian corn'. Never seen by Europeans, there was a belief that maize may turn early settlers into 'savages'. They steered clear,

opting instead for the imported Old World grain of rye, which fared well in the cooler north and mountainous regions of middle North America. The Scotch-Irish, already keen distillers, made quick use of equipment or knowledge brought from their homelands to knock up a makeshift still. Since whiskey preserved grain, these stills effectively turned surplus crops into tradable currency. These rye whiskies were the initial staples for the remote farming populace. However, another drink would long hold the title of top tipple in America.

AMERICAN RUM & BOURBON COUNTY

Whiskey was far from the most popular drink in America through the 17th century and up until the mid-18th century. New England, Boston and New York developed booming distillation industries, turning cheap Caribbean molasses into spirit. Massive shipments of rum were imported from the British island colonies. Friction between conflicting British and North American interests caused political tension that eventually led to war. 1775 saw the first hostilities. On 4 July 1776, the Declaration of Independence was signed and thirteen colonies banded together to fight. By 1783, with the French supporting American troops, Britain finally acknowledged American independence. With Caribbean imports impossible during the war, America had to once again become self-reliant for its drink fix.

With a whole population in need of strong booze, the whiskey industry really began to take off. 1774 had seen a settlement established at Fort Harrod, Virginia, which would later become Kentucky. Migration continued and those who went west, further inland, began making a distinctly different type of whiskey to the ryes of the east. In Kentucky, formed in 1792, the maize grew quickly, produced more flour when milled, and needed less care than rye. Just as their ancestors had done before them, farmers turned any surplus maize into whiskey. A huge landmass, named after a French royal family in honour of French aid to the United States during the Revolution, was formed in 1785. It was called Bourbon County. Transport was poor. Any whiskey which wasn't drunk by the locals was sent down the Mississippi River on flatboats from a port at Limestone. Bourbon County was greatly reduced in size after being split into many more counties. Still, it was affectionately referred to as Old Bourbon. When any whiskey was transported downriver to cities like New Orleans, the barrels would be labelled as 'Old Bourbon Whiskey'. Eventually, people began to think 'old' referred to the age of the whiskey. By this

'Always drink your whiskey with your gun hand, to show your friendly intentions.'

SCOTTISH
KLONDIKER'S
PROVERB

time the use of 'Old Bourbon' in reference to the place had died out.

Ageing wasn't yet widespread, but the time spent in barrels whilst being agitated in transit mellowed the flavour of the whiskey. The reputation garnered by maize-dominant whiskies meant people would ask for bourbon as a way of distinguishing corn whiskey from rye.

THE WHISKEY BOYS- A BOOZY REVOLT

By 1791 enough domestic whiskey was being produced that President George Washington saw fit to start taxing production. The tax sought to recoup the financial loss of war, although farm distillers saw it as an impingement on their freedom. When a Pennsylvanian excise officer tried to collect the tax, sixteen men dressed as women met him. The officer was tarred, feathered and sent on his way, with a clear message of resistance. It wasn't just the excise men who got a going-over. Any distillers who paid their taxes received similar treatment. Some would have their stills riddled with bullets. In honour of their handy work, still-shooters took on the moniker 'Tom the Tinker'. The situation boiled over in what is known as the Whiskey Rebellion, fought by the Whiskey Boys.

In 1794, after being served writs, rural Pennsylvanians rallied together against the tax. By the time they reached Pittsburgh they numbered 5,000 tax-opposing outlaws. President George Washington began to assemble an army, believing an example should be made of traitors against government. By the time the force was established the Whiskey Boys had been doing some thinking. They surrendered, but the message was heeded. In 1802 the tax was repealed. Interestingly enough, after his term in office Washington would go on to open his own rye distillery, with the help of a Scottish distiller.

The next hundred years of American whiskey production saw great advancements in transportation links and distillation techniques. This didn't translate into cheap good quality booze. Nefarious whiskey distributors and vendors used every manner of adulterant to make cheap unaged spirit resemble the aged efforts of quality distillers. Powerful conglomerates formed around these operations. The Whiskey Ring exemplified just how corrupt the business became. When the ring was investigated, the trail led to the Secretary of State stationed in the White House. Disbandment of the Whiskey Ring resulted in others taking their place. The 'Whiskey Trust' ran through the 1860s and

70s, selling inferior products at prices which undercut traditional bourbon distillers. These scams damaged the reputation of whiskey but prompted favourable action. George Gavin Brown, intent on selling medicinal whiskey, began bottling Old Forester bourbon in glass bottles from 1870. Bottles were harder to contaminate than barrels. The rest of the industry wouldn't follow suit until prohibition, when glass manufacture became cheaper thanks to industrialised production.

Thomas Shirley introduced the branding of bourbons as a mark of quality. The greatest battle won was the banding together of Kentucky distillers by Colonel Edmund Hayes Taylor to lobby against malpractice in defence of the reputation of bourbon. Efforts helped pass the Bottled in Bond Act of 1897 and the Pure Food and Drug Act, setting in place parameters which define bourbon to this day.

TEMPERANCE, PROHIBITION & THE ROAR OF THE 20S

Though many of the founders of the United States were as deeply devout to their drinking as they were to their religion, it was inevitable some would oppose the effects of alcohol. Americans reputedly drank morning till night. This concerned President Thomas Jefferson. He believed wine might be a better drink for the country than hard spirit. One Dr. Benjamin Rush shared his fears and wrote an essay voicing the potential destructive qualities of spirits, which he distributed as widely as he could. Ten years of repeat publication made an impression. The first American temperance society formed in New York in 1808. Others sprang up over the next century. They worked tirelessly, encouraging restrictions on state laws. By 1920, the USA was primed for prohibition.

Far from stopping consumption, the 'Great Experiment' served only to create a new culture of illicit drinking. Jazz-filled speakeasies flowed with illegal imports and homemade hooch alike. Cocktails became popularised as fruit juices and other ingredients masked foul booze. Prohibition created a market for criminal exploitation. Ringleaders such as Al Capone generated vast profits in booze smuggling. Corruption was rife. Judges, congressmen and police officers often turned a blind eye for the right price.

Regulation of alcohol was impossible. When authorities seized nearly 500,000 gallons of banned booze in 1928 they found 98% of it was toxic. But this didn't stop people drinking. New York City in 1927 had twice as many drinking joints than before prohibition. But the risk of drinking potentially poisonous alcohol had a silver lining – drinkers would ask for their choice drink by name, rather than by type. Foreign imports were a status symbol, a mark of sophistication as well as wealth. Women, who weren't typically found in legal saloons, flocked to speakeasies and drank in the same manner as men.

But the raucous parties and racketeering couldn't last. The Wall Street Crash of 1929 was catastrophic for the economy. One of the causes was prohibition itself. Lost revenues from alcohol taxation and the financial implications of policing prohibition are estimated at some 11 billion dollars over the 13 years of the Great Experiment. In 1933 President Franklin D. Roosevelt repealed prohibition. Americans were once again free to distil and drink bourbon.

While a large number of bourbon distilleries were forced to close during prohibition, some managed to survive, selling their whiskey as medicines. After the end of

The Second World War, the bourbon industry began to experience growth. Equipment was replenished from prohibition and producers had no military distractions. But from the 1970s bourbon started to experience rapid decline. Even today bourbon producers have had to diversify portfolios to become competitive. This isn't necessarily a bad thing. Many of the established brands have begun exploring their casks to find unique and select permutations of their product. Bourbon and rye production, though lacking invigoration, excels in consistency. A product unable to evolve often ceases to exist. But with bourbons and ryes, stubbornness has always been their strong suit. Hopefully they will be dealt better hands in the future.

'There is no such thing as bad whiskey. Some whiskies just happen to be better than others.'

WILLIAM
FAULKNER

THE BARTENDER'S
CHOICE

SPEED RAIL

Wild Turkey 101, 50.5%

If it was good enough for Hunter S. Thompson, I'll take a bottle and a night alone at my desk. A large part of drinking is, I feel, our ideas about what that drink represents. Some would say alcoholism – they'd make a valid point – but I also think this drink signifies a break away from the establishment. Hunter may not have been able to outdrink his demons (they'll always win), but he had great taste in attempting to do so. Deceptively smooth for its strength.

BACK BAR

Woodford Reserve Double Oaked, 43.2%

I've always loved this bourbon. The regular Woodford is grand, and it's great to see them experimenting, which too few established brands do. It's oaky and spicy, really offering a new dimension to an old fashioned. If you want a simple and plain old fashioned, give the regular Woodfords a go. You won't be disappointed.

TOP SHELF

Blanton's Straight from the Barrel, various strengths

Seasoned bourbon drinkers have been deprived of the idiosyncrasies of Scottish single malts. Slowly, bourbon producers are attempting to correct this. With Blanton's you can't really go wrong. You'll have your favourites, but anything they send up is going to be well crafted and well received.

3 WAYS

TO DRINK

BOURBON

OLD FASHIONED

50ml bourbon
4 dashes Angostura
bitters
1 sugar cube
dash soda

One of the oldest drinks in the book. Still a firm go-to; try varying the sugar amount to taste. Perfect after-dinner sipper.

› Place sugar cube in rocks glass
› Dash bitters onto sugar cube
› Pour a splash of soda onto the cube
› Crush and stir cube till dissolved (add a drop of whiskey to assist if necessary)
› Add bourbon and 2 cubes of ice
› Stir till ice has dissolved
› Top with ice
› Express orange peel over drink

NEW YORK SOUR

50ml bourbon
25ml lemon juice
20ml simple syrup
10ml red wine
4 mint leaves
1 egg white (use 1 for
two drinks)

Mint and whiskey and egg and wine?
Yep, really. I implore you to try it. Many
bartenders leave out the egg and mint and
float the wine on top. I don't, but I wouldn't
be upset with you if you did. For the less
adventurous, take out the mint and the
wine and you've got a perfect whiskey
sour. Now you're interested...

› Add all ingredients to shaker
› Dry shake for 13-15 seconds, taking
  care the shaker doesn't pop
› Add ice to the shaker and shake
  vigorously for 13-15 seconds
› Double strain into a chilled coupe or
  roman wine glass

OUT-OF-TOWNER

25ml bourbon
25ml Laird's applejack
12.5ml bianco vermouth
12.5ml dry vermouth
(I used Regal Rogue
Daringly Dry)
2 dashes Angostura
bitters

This twist on the Manhattan is a lighter,
more floral alternative to a classic.
Best sipped in the summer on a languid
afternoon.

› Begin chilling coupe glass
› Add all ingredients to mixing glass
› Add ice and stir until diluted and chilled
› Discard ice in coupe glass
› Strain drink into glass
› Express lemon twist over drink
  and discard

'Too much of anything is bad, but too much good whiskey is barely enough.'

MARK
TWAIN

CURIOSITIES

The colour of bourbon, just like any other whiskey, comes from the process of barrel ageing. When any whiskey comes off a still, it is colourless. Not until the "green" whiskey has spent time in a barrel does it begin to extract colour, tannins and vanillin (the molecule responsible for notes of butter, caramel, banana, coconut and, of course, vanilla) from the wood.

Since it was the sale of alcohol that was banned during prohibition and not possession, bourbon producers found themselves in an interesting predicament. Many had warehouses with millions of gallons of barrel-ageing bourbon, which was locked up by the government but that they technically still owned. Some distillers turned to stealing their own stock in order to sell it on the black market.

Throughout The Second World War, US bourbon distilleries began making alcohol exclusively for the war effort. They produced over 1.2 billion gallons of alcohol, used to make everything from synthetic rubber and plastics to explosives and antifreeze.

R U M

For all of rum's sweetness, the drink has a bitter past. From colonialist beginnings, rum became a prized commodity, which helped perpetuate the slave and fur trades. The drink offered escapism to enslaved people and sailors. But there was much that this alcoholic brew, for all its reputed medicinal effects, couldn't salve. The spirit of rum has since emerged, synonymous with relaxation and vacation. Rum is often the key ingredient in Tiki-style cocktails, which transport us, even in the coldest climes, to warmer shores and shimmering seas.

WHAT IS RUM?

Rum is produced by fermenting sugar cane juice, or molasses, a thick syrupy by-product of sugar making. Rum is made on six of the seven continents, but the majority of rums come from the Caribbean and South America. That said, it's difficult to give a further definition of rum as there are so many variables in production styles and techniques, from the grassy, sweet rhum agricole, to the ripe banana of dunder (stillage)-heavy Jamaican styles. Rums can be unaged, or aged in barrels, with some of the oldest having seen 50 years in casks. Rum strengths also vary tremendously from 37.5% right up to around 85% ABV. A simplified guide to rum styles would be:

Light rums are unaged or have spent very little time in barrels. They range from colourless to a light straw colour.

Gold rums spend varying time in barrels and may or may not be coloured with additions such as caramels. Their hues range from light gold to deep, rich, ruddy-amber.

Dark rums have been aged and often have caramels added to give them their dark colouration.

Spiced rums are usually aged and cut with fruit peels and spices, such as cloves and all-spice berries. They also generally tend to be sweetened.

SWEET GRASS

There are over 30 varieties of sugar cane, a perennial member of the grass family, classified under the name Saccharum officinarum. Grown in China and many surrounding countries by 6,000 BCE, it is thought the plant was first cultivated in New Guinea as early as 8,000 BCE. The earliest record of sugar cane fermentation emerges from India around 3,800 years ago, in a manuscript known as 'Book of the Happy State of Mind', or Manasollana. Sugar cane was first introduced to Europeans when Alexander the Great's general encountered 'honey without the help of bees' in 326 CE India. His attempts to bring the tropical plant back to Greece failed. The grass couldn't survive Mediterranean conditions.

By the Middle Ages sugar cane was highly coveted. Christian traders bartered with Muslims from the Middle East and Africa. No longer content with trading to supply a growing demand for sugar across the continent, the Christians of Europe sought to find land where sugar cane could be grown. In the late

1400s, they finally found a paradise for the plant.

THE EARLY COLONISATION OF SOUTH AMERICA & THE CARIBBEAN

The year 1492 represents a paradigm in human history. The Muslim Moors, from a blend of geographies ranging from Africa to the Middle East, were expelled from Granada. They had brought religion and rule but also science, mathematics, medicine and a tolerance of other religion (at the price of a higher tax). In the same year, on 12 October, Christopher Columbus landed on what he thought were the East Indies. He found the Bahamas, the Greater Antilles and the northern archipelago of the Lesser Antilles, governed by people known as the Taíno. A smaller population, the Caribs, populated islands in the southern Lesser Antilles. With one exception, they received Columbus peacefully, as Columbus took the measure of their gold earrings and military capabilities. Columbus' second voyage the following year saw him take numerous crops: tobacco, grapevines, and a crop never before seen in the Caribbean, sugar cane. The vessels also carried materials and people to populate the new Spanish colonies. The Portuguese followed, claiming their own islands along with part of the Brazilian mainland.

Spanish settlers were initially disgruntled by the lack of promised gold. In the early 1500s, the Portuguese occupied themselves with sugar production, a skill honed in African colonies. However, the scale of work proved too much for the indentured servants and early settlers of Brazil. Attempts at Native American enslavement resulted in rebellion, successful because of their

'Fifteen men on the dead man's chest –
...Yo-ho-ho, and a bottle of rum!
Drink and the devil had done for the rest –
...Yo-ho-ho, and a bottle of rum!'

ROBERT LOUIS
STEVENSON

knowledge of their homeland, or death. The indigenous succumbed to diseases for which they had no immunity. As such, enslaved people were purchased from Arab traders in Africa and shipped to the new colonies as a source of labour.

Initially these were criminals, prisoners of war or people who couldn't pay debts. Slavery was no new concept. Enslaved people and indentured servants had been used for thousands of years. Even as late as the 1640s English slaves in Africa outnumbered black slaves in the West Indies. But demand for slaves to drive productivity would create an unparalleled market for human abduction. It was the first time in history enslaved people were used as part of a scalable economic model. The capitalist experiment led to astronomical profits and a humanitarian catastrophe. By 1807 over 3.1 million Africans would have

been taken as slaves by the British alone, of whom only 2.7 million would actually survive to reach their destination. Among other ends, many would jump to their death in the sea rather than become a tradable commodity. And one of the top items on the trading itinerary was rum.

'KILL-DEVIL' & EARLY DISTILLATION

The British and French soon found sun-drenched islands of their own. The British stumbled upon Barbados in 1607 and by 1627 had a settlement in Holetown. Martinique became home to a French colony in 1635. In an attempt to generate income, cotton, indigo and tobacco were planted, but nothing grew as well in the climate as sugar cane.

In the first quarter of the 1600s colonists and captives alike had a thirst for alcoholic drinks. Fermented brews suppressed the horrors Africans endured but they also offered a way to preserve the brewing traditions of their homeland. People fermented anything they could, including cassava and sweet potato. Palm trees were utilised to make palm wine – a drink that played a large part in West African societies when giving libations to the gods. Enslaved people also made keen use of the skim-off from sugar cauldrons and molasses, which was initially seen as a useless waste product, fed to cattle or made into inferior sugar. Colonist settlers also experimented with pineapples, plantains, bananas and oranges. This inclination towards brews coupled with knowledge of distillation went towards creating the first rums.

Rum was being distilled in Barbados as early as 1631, with rums reported in Martinique around 1640. Brazil at that time dominated the sugar industry. From the 1640s onward Barbados followed Brazil's example – sugar cane became the principal crop, for which every spare piece of land was prioritised. Incidentally, it may have been temporary Dutch command of northern Brazil which resulted in the making of cachaça – Brazilian rum distilled from the ferment of sugar cane juice rather than molasses.

As a matter of course, Bajan sugar cane plantations were equipped with distilleries, often run by enslaved distillers. Britain's acquisition of Jamaica from the Spanish in 1655 led to more production. Rum became akin to currency both at home and abroad. And of course, much was drunk by colonists themselves. Since 'eau de vie de cannes', as it was known in Martinique, or 'kill-devil' among British colonists, was still believed to possess medicinal benefits, rum was drunk to fend off any number of ailments on the islands.

In the cold Caribbean nights, if the apothecary feared slaves might catch a chill, they were dispensed rum to fight off the cold. Other owners were less caring. Calorific rum would supplement substantial meals to provide the slaves with a cheap source of energy. Though rum production was fairly well established, in the 1650s only 10-15% of the rum produced in Barbados was exported. Inhabitants consumed the rest. Under trying conditions fights would often break out. This is where we get the word rum, from the English rumbullion, meaning 'a great tumult'.

PIRATES, NAVAL RATIONING & A SEA OF RUM

By the end of the 1600s rum was beginning to establish itself along the Atlantic trade routes. This began with sailors. Whatever rum remained after a thirsty journey could be traded elsewhere. The main supplier of rum was Barbados, and their best customer North America. A 1676 ban on grain distillation in North America meant distillers had to find a new substance to distil. 19% of total Barbadian exports were rum between 1699 and 1701, but the percentage was higher for exported molasses. The Americans had cottoned on to making their own rum.

Similarly, French colonies from Canada to Louisiana received a decent dose of French colonial rum. French and British Caribbean rum was invaluable to fur traders. Strong booze ravaged Native American populations, though trading rum and whiskey with indigenous people was often banned. Spanish colonies had the potential to produce rum. Thankfully, those in positions of power had concerns about the effects of spirit consumption – especially on the indigenous population. By 1693, the

Spanish Crown had issued a ban on rum production. But this was far from an entirely noble act. The Spanish, French and Portuguese had their own alcohol industries back home to protect. The British, with no viable alcohol source such as brandy or wine, and with growing concerns towards gin drinking, stood to profit a great deal from the production of rum.

With so much valuable rum bobbing on the seas, opportunists were bound to take advantage. Pirates only roamed the Caribbean seas in two short bursts – the 1660s and the early years of the 1700s – no doubt thanks to occupational hazards. The romance we depict pirates with in popular culture often masks heinous crimes. Sir Henry Morgan, whose name might sound familiar, was a mercenary for King Charles II. Morgan's deal was as follows: in return for attacking Spanish ships in Columbia or Cuba, he

was entitled to pay himself from any treasure retrieved. Business was profitable, but Morgan's methods proved ruthless beyond being useful to Blighty. In 1670 a state of truce was reached between Britain and Spain in Panama. Morgan and his men took it upon themselves to torch the city. Morgan was arrested and extradited back to Britain under charges of piracy. Amazingly, though in direct defiance of foreign policy, he was not only acquitted but subsequently received a knighthood. It was bearing this title that he accepted the role of deputy governor in Jamaica, where he lived out his days, drinking rum until it killed him.

The competition North American rum presented for the British, whose interests were firmly rooted in selling their own Caribbean rum, gave London cause to lobby for the Molasses Act in 1733. The act doubled duties on exported molasses, but rather than paying the imposed tax, North American distillers simply bought contraband molasses from elsewhere. This led to the Sugar Act of 1764. If the British Royal Navy suspected a ship of harbouring illicit cargo of sugar, rum or molasses, it could board the ship and acquire any items deemed illegal. Effectively this gave the British legitimate powers of piracy. Mounting political tensions led the North American colonists to unite against the British. Following almost a decade of fighting, the United States would have their freedom.

In Britain throughout the 1700s rum became a fashionable alternative to the evils of gin drinking. The government saw rum as an opportunity to capitalise on the spirits market, which France and Spain had dominated till then. The spirit was an exotic luxury for aspirational Brits who couldn't afford imported brandy or wine from continental Europe. While spirit drinking was causing concern, even 1750s Britain perceived rum as healthier than gin or brandy. The formal rationing of alcohol to the British Army and Navy in 1731 served only to fuel demand. The official ration was a gallon of daily beer but rum could be offered as a substitute. Further to this, the government made rum an indispensable part of Royal Navy rations in 1775. It wouldn't be until 1970 that this was revised.

REBELLION, ABOLITION AND TEMPERANCE

Several factors contributed to the end of the slave trade, which led to a downturn in the production of rum. Though there'd been many Christian objectors since slavery began, profits had nullified their voices. Likewise, those in the business of buying and selling humans had duly ignored rebellions. From the onset of the triangular slave trade, African kingdoms had fought off abductors and sent unheeded messages of appeal to European courts. On ships that crossed the Middle Passage from Western Africa to the West Indies, the people whose lives had been paid for in rum often rebelled. It was expected that 1 in 10 ships would see prisoners rise up against their captors. When vessels reached their destination, rebel factions escaped and formed. These coordinated substantial Maroon forces, which frequently engaged in combat against colonists.

The great turning point in the slave trade was the rebel liberation of St. Domingue. The land captured by these newly-freed women and men became Haiti. More and more profits were lost to quelling resistance, and pressure from abolitionists mounted on both sides of the Atlantic. The slave trade was abolished in 1808, although slavery in that part of the world was only officially outlawed in 1834. It would take many more years for Britain to acknowledge that slavery was unacceptable in other territories of the East India Company. In Sierra Leone it wouldn't be until 1928 that slavery was reluctantly abolished under pressure from the League of Nations. Even in the Caribbean, ex-slave owners still profited. Countries like Haiti were forced to reimburse colonist countries for profits lost. In today's money these debts ran into the tens of billions.

The impact abolition had on rum production was drastic. Indentured servants were called in from other colonies globally to continue production. However, changing attitudes towards rum drinking in the Caribbean, along with associations of slavery with rum in Europe, lowered supply and demand. Through the late 1800s a new wave of European Christian missionaries flocked to the Caribbean. Their teachings of temperance created some strange effects. In the 1890s, Jamaica, with a heavy influx of Christian influence, produced the most rum, while the island consumed the least. Barbados on the other hand, where production had plummeted, still consumed great quantities, since they'd received less missionary influence.

FROM PAIN TO PLEASURE

Throughout the early 20th century, American prohibition increased alcohol production in the Caribbean. Prohibition helped popularise cocktails, not only in the US but abroad, where American holidaymakers could savour their drinks without fear of the law. For those US citizens who couldn't afford a trip, there were plenty of facilitators rum-running untold quantities of alcohol. Following the Great Experiment, the likes of Humphrey Bogart and Charlie Chaplin could be found at a new Hollywood bar, which was serving up a flamboyant and unique style of cocktail. At Don the Beachcomber's, rum was a key ingredient in the Tiki drinks that Ernest Gantt invented.

Between the middle to last quarter of the 1900s, vodka and gin replaced rum as the favoured spirit. Over the past three decades, however, rum has had a renaissance. Tiki-inspired bars, as well as the emergence of newly marketed spiced rums and some truly sublime sipping rums, have popularised the drink across a broad spectrum of people. India drinks the most rum on the planet, drunk neat, with ice, or cut with cola. Rum's pairing with cola or other mixers and its ubiquity across the globe has often seen its reputation tainted as a common drink. But this image is changing. Among industry enthusiasts and bartenders alike rum has reached the status of cognacs and scotches, savoured as a drink of refinement. Perhaps more than any other drink rum manages to appeal to all, finding favour everywhere from dancehalls to rum babas at fine dining restaurants.

From slavery to the hardships of life on the waves, rum has been both comfort to and catalyst for difficult times in history. Echoes of those times still ripple across the pond of consciousness. The spirit itself has emerged triumphant, championed by some as the most flavourful and versatile of distillates. With so much history and the ability to conjure far-off places, it is easy to see why rum has become a global favourite.

THE BARTENDER'S
CHOICE

SPEED RAIL

Flor de Caña 4 Year Old Extra Dry Rum, 40%
Exactly what you wouldn't expect from a rum.
This really tasty offering from Nicaragua is
decent on its own, but mixed up in a daiquiri
it's a dream.

BACK BAR

Smith and Cross, 57%
Bottled at navy-strength, this fantastic rum
from Jamaica has all the funky banana notes
you'd expect from the island. Top quality
single-pot still rum that's difficult to put down
till it knocks you over.

TOP SHELF

El Dorado 15 Year Special Reserve, 43%
This Guyanese expression is an absolute
corker. Bang-on sip from a great distillery.
A 'yes' every single time.

3WAYS

TODRINK

RUM

MOJITO

50ml white rum
25ml lime juice
15-20ml sugar syrup
8-10 mint leaves
25ml soda

Meaning 'little spell' or 'little magic'. A common misconception is that the mint needs to be muddled. The menthol sacs on the underside of the leaves are sensitive enough to open at an insect's touch. Stirring with a spoon imparts plenty of flavour, whereas tearing by muddling releases bitter sap into the drink.

› Add all ingredients except soda to hi-ball / Collins glass
› Fill 2/3 with crushed ice
› Stir thoroughly, distributing leaves throughout the glass
› Top with crushed ice (pressing ice into glass)
› Add soda
› Cap with ice, add a straw and garnish with a mint sprig

MAI-TAI

20ml Martinique gold
rum
20ml Jamaican gold rum
20ml Bajan gold rum
10ml Cointreau
15ml orgeat syrup
(almond)
25ml lime juice

The name for this comes from the
Hawaiian word for 'the greatest' or
'champion'. I couldn't agree more.

› Add all ingredients to shaker
› Shake vigorously for 12-15 seconds
› Double strain into a double
  old fashioned glass
› Add fresh ice
› Add straw and garnish with a mint sprig,
  cocktail cherry and orange wedge

BUBBLE RUM

INGREDIENTS

35ml white rum
(Flor de Caña extra dry
4 years is tasty here)
10ml fresh lime
30ml fresh grapefruit
10ml sugar syrup
Top with champagne

Super refreshing and super simple.

› Add all ingredients except champagne to
  a shaker
› Add ice and shake thrice
› Double strain into chilled cocktail coupe
› Express grapefruit peel over drink and
  discard
› Enjoy, while thinking of beaches

'It was a maddening image and the only
way to whip it was to hang on until dusk
and banish the ghosts with rum.'

HUNTER S.
THOMPSON

CURIOSITIES

After suffering a fatal sniper wound in the 1805 Battle of Trafalgar, Lord Horatio Nelson's body was transported in rum to preserve it for the journey home. The crew couldn't quite fight their thirsts and most of the rum was gone by the time the cask reached England. Navy rum was thereafter named 'Nelson's Blood', a term still used today.

Bacardi hasn't been made in Cuba since 1960 when Fidel Castro nationalised the company, forcing many of the Bacardi family into exile. The family still run the company but the rum itself is made in Puerto Rico.

The term 'proof' as a measure of alcohol comes from the practice of mixing rum with gunpowder to see if the alcohol still lit (this happens if alcohol is over 57% ABV). One reason was to check sailors weren't being swindled with poor rum. But it also meant that on a ship storing both rum and gunpowder, if there was an accident with a barrel, crews could still fire their armaments.

GIN

Initially a key ingredient or pleasant accompaniment to remedies, gin has played both the villain and the hero through its life, often at the same time. The story of gin is a dizzying draught of naval exploration, medicine, politics and class spanning nearly five centuries. How could a drink that initially had its roots in alchemy, have created such a great impact in such a short space of time?

WHAT IS GIN?

Gin is made by distilling a neutral grain spirit with juniper berries and other botanicals. Often this distillate is redistilled to refine the drink but occasionally gin makers opt for simply macerating the ingredients in a neutral spirit which is then diluted to the desired strength and bottled. The taste profile of gins can differ tremendously but the defining feature of gin is juniper. Most gins generally use five to ten botanicals to impart flavour and aroma but producers have been known to use well over forty. Some of the most common ingredients found in gins are: angelica root and seeds, orris root, coriander seeds, grain of paradise, cassia bark, cinnamon, ginger, cardamom, almond, cubeb berries, nutmeg, lemon peel, orange peel, sage, rosemary, lavender, basil and bay. The strengths of gin also vary greatly but modern gins are

often bottled between 37.5-43% ABV.

THE GIN CRAZE- EXCESSIVE CONSOLATION

After an age of infancy and development by alchemists in the Middle East, distilled spirit found its way to Europe where it was often paired with plentiful juniper berries to preserve their medicinal properties past season. While not yet known as gin, these juniper spirits offered a new preservation method. Remedies became annually accessible – a relationship gin would come to honour later. People, being people, also enjoyed the non-medical effects of these elixirs and gradually consumption became both medicinal and recreational.

Eventually genever, the Dutch spirit flavoured with juniper, began to be produced in Holland. Well before absinthe took artists on their flights of inspirational fancy, the heralded 'Lady Genever' found her way to Britain from the Netherlands. British tongues simply named her gin. In 1688 James II was usurped by William of Orange, who hailed from the Dutch Republic. Shortly after, the 1690 Act raised duties on French wine and brandy, while allowing anyone to distil gin if they purchased a cheap license and gave short notice. The gin craze had begun.

Embraced by the poorer classes in Britain, gin production exploded, first to the benefit and then to the horror of the government and upper classes. For the first time in history a limitless torrent of cheap, strong booze was available to the masses of London. Previously, people had cheered their poor souls with small beer. Gin, however, exotic to the untravelled English and potent as poison, won the hearts of the impoverished. At this time in London slums even children were given weak beer in place of water because it was safer. People did get drunk on beer but gin was a different beast and little was understood about the long-term effects of strong alcohol consumption. Demand was unprecedented and some distilleries started adding ingredients, such as turpentine and sulphuric acid, to the pot stills. The quantities served by taverns and proprietors were as unthinkable by modern standards as the absence of ice. A newspaper expressing dismay at a sign outside a gin shop reported the advertisement:

Drunk for 1d. Dead drunk for 2d. Clean straw for nothing.

What that meant was a quarter pint for a penny, a half pint for two pennies, and if you found the room was spinning a little too fast, you could nap on some clean straw for free. With the gin craze in full flow on the streets of London, chilling stories began to emerge.

Here a mother had killed her child, selling the clothes to buy gin. There wet nurses took juniper cordials for the infant's benefit, became addicted, and neglected the young in their care. One was dropped on a fire. Others starved in cribs as their stewards slumped in a ginny stupor. Another story tells of how a man charged with killing his mother in a gin-clouded rage was acquitted on the premise he was not in his right mind.

The government launched a moral crusade against 'Mother's Ruin' with the first gin act. Mourners draped in black held processions for the death of 'Lady Genever'. Not altogether banned, the license cost had become virtually unaffordable. However, rather than killing off gin, the act drove production underground, doing little to put punters' palates off their swig of choice. This near-prohibition led to some tales of delightful ingenuity. The contraption made by Dudley Bradstreet, a sign in the form of a painted cat named Old Tom, was used to dispense gin under its paw through a pipe. Buyers popped their money into a drawer whilst whispering the incantation, 'Puss, give me two penny-worth of gin'. After a moment's wait, out the gin flowed!

Heightened moral attitudes meant people were horrified by gin and saw it as the embodiment of evil. Mounting pressure in government led to several redrafts of the Gin Acts, yet few were successful. Eventually the 1743 Gin Act found a recipe to curb consumption, lowering the cost of a licence while increasing duties. Customers paid more for gin and licensed premises took the place of underground suppliers. The gin craze had finally been quelled and appetites for gin diminished with it.

In 18th-century Britain, gin can be seen as a nuanced symbol of class divides. On the one hand it offered consolation to a downtrodden class, while also bringing about their destruction. On the other it gave the government a ferocious income for the country, at the same time throwing up questions of morality, class mobility and hypocrisy. Behind the doors of townhouses many a bottle of wine and brandy were sunk. For a country that less than a generation on would be one of the greatest powers in the world, Britain had become an example of the implications of unchecked spirit drinking.

THE G&T

Arguably, in England the gin and tonic is the go-to after beer. In the same way you might have an Aperol spritz in Italy, caipirinhas in Brazil, margaritas in Mexico or Manhattans in New York; to visit England (especially London), without the indulgence of a G&T would be a missed trick.

'Gin and drugs, dear lady, gin and drugs.'

T . S . E L I O T
*when asked where to find inspiration

But how did the gin and tonic, with its unmistakable luminosity in the black light of clubs, become such a staple of English culture?

The answer, as often is the case with Britain's relationship with booze, lies with the military. From the early 1800s British troops and sailors were advised to drink quinine with spirit or wine to help protect them against malaria in the tropics. In the middle of the 19th century, British colonies used the addition of gin to make the newly developed carbonated Indian tonic water more palatable. Needless to say, the gin also helped lift the spirits of men destined to spend months away from their families. It wasn't too long before the taste for a G&T travelled back to Britain and the grand hotels of the West End began serving its patrons tonic to complement their fragrant spirit.

PROHIBITION AND BEYOND

After the gin craze, 'Mother's Ruin' fell somewhat out of favour with the Brits. Charles Dickens was publicly dismissive of excessive gin drinking, which didn't stop him having a few cheeky fingers in private. Whilst the arrival of drinks such as the gin and tonic made quaffing gin in public more acceptable, it wasn't until adoption by the US during prohibition that 'Mother Gin' got a face lift. The 'Great Experiment' that ran from 1920 to 1933 gave the Dutch lady, who had a less romantic, if no less passionate relationship with Britain, a new life.

Cocktail culture had popularised the spirit in the States but it was the underground speakeasies which gave it glamour. Gin was a popular choice as it was a lot simpler to make illegally produced liquor taste like gin than to try and mimic the aged taste of whisky or brandy with caramel. Gin's forbidden romance with the US made it cultured and cool. The drink once again represented something exotic, with sweet and dry vermouths from the continent being married with the stylised London dry gin in American bars.

Not only did the liquor captivate the public, it also cultivated an important relationship with artists. Until then, most writing about gin had been cautionary and moralistic, but in North America, writers and film makers seemed to have acquired a taste for the spirit. It would be nigh impossible to have a conversation about early 20th-century literary giants F. Scott Fitzgerald and Ernest Hemingway without mentioning their propensity for drink. It was rumoured Fitzgerald favoured gin because the smell wouldn't be detected on his breath. Hemingway was known to pride himself on his adept martini making – he was so particular he'd freeze his cocktail onions to -15°C to keep his drink as cold as possible.

During North American prohibition gin again led a double life. Publicly it was outlawed but behind the closed doors of even the most respectable citizens, gin was being chilled and swilled. It is said that President Franklin D. Roosevelt made the first legal (albeit poorly-made) martinis when he revoked prohibition. Cabinet members complained that Roosevelt overdid it with the vermouth when whipping up a batch of the cocktail. Perhaps he could be forgiven because he'd forgotten how to make them – were it not for the fact his council had commented on the president's mixing capabilities before the repeal of prohibition too.

Literature, film and the cocktail party, which took off after the end of prohibition, all helped to make the clear, bright spirit popular again in Blighty. Winston Churchill was said to take his martinis all-gin, with either a bottle of vermouth in the room, or a bow in the direction of France. But gin's largest leap into popular culture was when it found itself in the hands of a spy. It wasn't until James Bond first ordered a Vesper in *Casino Royale* that the martini became iconic.

Fast forward to today and we have seen an explosion in the market. Gin has become synonymous with craft culture and artisan production. Like no other spirit before it, gin has spurred a flurry of small distillers. In Britain the number of gin distilleries has more than doubled since 2010.

The spirit of gin is forever reviving itself. In its life gin has played enemy to the state while somehow remaining endorsed by it, swigged by the downtrodden and sipped by high society. Many have used it as an elixir to alleviate their burdens, others to elevate parties to their zenith. While the history of gin is rarely as clear as the liquid, it is never less fragrant. A complex mix of ingredients with the water of life at its heart.

'I like to have a martini,
Two at the very most.
After three I'm under the table,
after four I'm under my host.'

DOROTHY
PARKER

THE BARTENDER'S
CHOICE

SPEED RAIL

Sipsmith London Dry Gin, 41.6%

I've loved this gin since I tried it and can't
really stop going back to it. Lovely hit of juniper
without being overpowering.
Often my pick for a martini.

BACK BAR

Jensen Old Tom Gin, 43%

Tasty introduction to the Old Tom style of
gin for those who aren't acquainted. This
is basically the missing link between Dutch
genever and London dry gin.
Really decent in a Martinez cocktail.

TOP SHELF

Junipero, 49.3%

Unlike many of the newer gins on the market,
Junipero is unashamedly juniper-forward, which
funnily enough is what I really dig in a gin. If I could
have a lifetime supply of a gin, it would be this.

3 WAYS

TO DRINK GIN

INGREDIENTS

25ml gin (preferably
London dry)
25ml sweet vermouth
(experiment with
different brands –
differences are dramatic)
25ml Campari

NEGRONI

Ah, the ubiquitous Negroni. One fateful
date between 1919 and 1920, Count
Negroni was having a bad day. He
stopped by the Caffè Casoni and
asked his bartender mate Fosco Scarselli
to fix him up something stronger than
the popular Americano cocktail. Fosco
substituted soda water for gin and the
Negroni was born.

› Add all ingredients to mixing glass
› Fill with ice and stir till chilled and
  sufficiently diluted
› Strain into rocks glass
› Add fresh ice
› Express oils of orange peel – get right into
  the drink with this, it's strong enough to
  carry that orange flavor

THE LAST WORD

20ml gin
20ml green Chartreuse
20ml Maraschino
Liqueur
20ml lime juice

I don't have a favourite cocktail, but if you really pushed me to name just one, it's likely I'd pick this. Complex, refreshing and balanced, I think it's a great example of what a well-made cocktail can be.

› Begin chilling coupe glass with ice
› Add all ingredients to shaker
› Shake hard for 12-15 seconds
› Discard ice in coupe and double strain drink into glass
› Garnish with a cherry

MORENO BABY

25ml London dry gin
25ml Martini Bianco
25ml lime juice
20ml apple juice
15ml orgeat syrup
3 mint leaves
2 slices cucumber

My co-worker Andrea Moreno, artist, ceramist and chef, used to love this drink. After creating her first street-food pop-up, Caracas Baby, she was feeling a bit flush. She ordered three Coolcumbers (my original name for the drink) in about 15 minutes and left via the rear fire exit singing.

› Add all ingredients to cocktail shaker
› Shake as hard as possible for 12-15 seconds
› Double strain into a chilled cocktail glass
› Garnish with cucumber, sliced to perch on glass

'The gin and tonic has saved more
Englishmen's lives, and minds,
than all the doctors in the Empire.'

WINSTON
CHURCHILL

CURIOSITIES

Two of the most evocative and famous pieces of art to emerge from the 18th century were William Hogarth's *Beer Street* and *Gin Lane*. Inspired by the gin craze, they were rendered as a warning of the effects of gin drinking.

The term 'Dutch Courage' comes from English soldiers' admiration for the bravery shown on the battlefield by Dutch soldiers pepped up on genever.

The largest consumer of gin in the world is the Philippines. The Philippine market accounts for well over a third of global gin consumption. Interestingly, the brand of gin drunk most in the Philippines, Ginebra San Miguel, most Westerners haven't even heard of!

ABSINTHE

Notorious beyond compare and a reputed stimulant for creativity, absinthe captured the world's imagination. From humble roots as a medicinal tonic in Switzerland, the Green Fairy spread to the boulevards of Paris. Absinthe became the source of inspiration for a whole movement of *absintheurs*. But this incredible popularity was short lived. The ban on absinthe in several countries around the globe meant the spirit was nearly lost. Why did absinthe become so popular? And what led to such fear that the drink nearly disappeared?

WHAT IS ABSINTHE?

Absinthe is a distilled spirit primarily flavoured with what is known as 'the holy trinity': green anise, sweet fennel and grand wormwood (*Artemisia absinthium*). The drink is named after the French for the latter plant: 'grande absinthe'. Other herbs and botanicals often used as ingredients include petite wormwood, calamus,

star anise, hyssop, coriander, angelica and veronica.

Absinthe is made by macerating chosen botanicals in a high-proof neutral spirit. The maceration is then distilled so the plant oils and alcohol are evaporated from the water and solid plant mass. The 'blanche' style of

absinthe, which is completely colourless, aromatic and full-flavoured, would then be bottled. The more widely known style of green or 'verte' absinthe requires a second maceration with fresh botanicals. This not only imparts further flavour and aroma but also gives the drink its hypnotic colour from the chlorophyll of the plants. Absinthe is traditionally bottled without sugar at high strength, typically around 55%-72% ABV. The intention is for this high alcohol percentage to be diluted with the addition of water (and sugar if preferred). When absinthe is diluted with water it loses its clarity, turning cloudy and opalescent in a phenomenon known as 'the louche'.

THE GREEN FAIRY

The key ingredient in absinthe, grand wormwood or Artemisia absinthium, is a perennial plant indigenous to Europe, Asia and several African countries. Also known as mugwort, it has been used for millennia for its curative powers. Ancient Egyptian scrolls documented on papyrus tell of its medicinal benefits 1,500 years before Christ. Its use assumedly reaches back much further. It was said to remedy a host of ailments including headaches, gout, fever and kidney stones, and later was used as a treatment for malaria. It could be burned to rid houses and clothes of pests such as fleas and moths. And, ironically, since small amounts were used to keep wine from deteriorating, grand wormwood was also said to have a sobering effect on those who had drunk one too many cups.

The name absinthium is derived from the Greek word apsinthion, meaning undrinkable. The plant has an exceptionally bitter taste – almost unpalatable unless tempered with water (or wine). The English term wormwood developed after sufferers with intestinal worms were given it as treatment. The active ingredient in grand wormwood is thujone. Thujone is a cousin of menthol and small quantities are naturally present in common foods like sage. In high quantities thujone becomes toxic causing convulsions and can lead to death – a fact which becomes crucial later in absinthe's history. Green anise and fennel are both members of the *apiaceae* family and bring flavours of aniseed and sweet liquorice. Anise, long believed to be an aphrodisiac, was sure to find its way into an alcoholic potion at some point.

Absinthe initially followed this medicinal heritage. Some claim the inventor of absinthe to be a French Huguenot doctor with a remarkably memorable name, Pierre Ordinaire. The myth goes, in exile from persecution, Ordinaire took refuge in Val de Travers, Switzerland. There he concocted absinthe as a cure for any ailment. Ordinaire travelled on horseback dispensing his green elixir, which developed a reputation. So impressed were the imbibers by the seemingly magic powers of the herbaceous tonic, they started referring to it as 'la Fée Verte', or the Green Fairy. It's said that before Ordinaire's death, he benevolently gave the recipe to two loyal customers, the Henriod sisters from Couvet, who kept up the doctor's work.

Thereafter, one Major Dubied fell under the spell of the fairy. He decided to buy the recipe from the sisters in 1797, with a view to producing it as an aperitif. A tidy beginning, this story, but as often with spirits, nothing is so simple. It appears absinthe was being distilled before Ordinaire even arrived in Switzerland. It's a possibility the Henriod sisters were the ones to introduce the French doctor to the drink in the first place. In Neuchâtel there was a tradition of pairing wormwood and other herbs with distillate stretching back well over half a century. Ordinaire then, was more a spirited promoter of la Fée Verte than an inventor – perhaps its very first ambassador.

Major Dubied returned to France with the Henriods' special recipe and enlisted the help of his son in law, Henri-Louis Pernod. They began modest production of absinthe under the company name of Maison Pernod Fils. Henri-Louis would go on to create a dynasty. War helped increase demand for absinthe. It was advantageous to distillers that spirits held a greater concentration of alcohol percentage over weaker drinks like beer and wine. This meant they were easily transported. The purported medicinal qualities of absinthe, especially its reputed effects against malaria, made it popular with the Troupes coloniales. Absinthe's unusually high bottling strength also helped to make it the choice

tipple for troops. Returning soldiers brought back a taste for absinthe, but the drink was also cultivating an independent following back home. A unique cocktail of characteristics made absinthe just as desirable to French civilians who hadn't been called upon to serve their country.

THE LOUCHE, CEREMONY AND HALLUCINOGENIC RUMOURS

Absinthe's high alcoholic strength, some over 70%, serves a purpose. The alcohol chemically traps the essential oils of plants, captured during distillation and steeping. When water is added these are released, turning the jewel-like clarity of the liquid cloudy. The process is known as the louche and makes present nuanced aromas and flavours that would otherwise remain locked in the alcohol. This is why absinthe is cut with very little or no water before bottling.

Diluting the strength of the absinthe and sweetening it with a sugar cube eventually developed into a ritual. A dose of absinthe would be poured into a glass, often marked with a measure. A perforated spoon was placed on top of the glass followed by a sugar cube. Finally, iced water was meticulously dripped or poured onto the cube, causing it to dissolve. As the liquid level rose, the louche took effect, creating galactic swirls until the drink became milky-green and opaque at a general ratio of 1:3, absinthe to water.

The aesthetes of cosmopolitan France found this ritual irresistible. All manner of accoutrements were developed to facilitate the process. Beautiful, multi-faceted absinthe fountains and spoons resembling the Eiffel Tower, erected in 1887, are still highly collectable. Absinthe drinking led to a cultish following of fanatical *absintheurs*. These were absinthe practitioners with yogi-like status amongst the café patrons of Paris. They would instruct those less versed in absinthe drinking on exactly how to prepare the mixture, sometimes charging a small fee for their wisdom. Montmartre became the epicentre of café culture and held theatre to hosts of writers and artists seeking inspiration. So popular was the Green Fairy as a pre-dinner drink, the time between 5pm and 6pm became known as *L'Heure Verte*, The Green Hour.

Attractive too were the reported effects of absinthe drinking. Contrary to popular belief, absinthe doesn't have any hallucinogenic properties. Some absinthe devotees do report a vivid drunkenness and clarity of vision, along with sharpened sensitivity and creative thoughts – though many others don't experience this phenomenon. Until very recently this has always been attributed to the thujone in wormwood.

But since this is only found in very small amounts, scientists now believe the blend of active ingredients in many of the herbs found in absinthe contributes to this effect. The art, literature and actions of prominent absinthe drinkers, along with exaggerations and embellishments in stories, all contributed to absinthe's drug-like status. The end of the Franco-Prussian war in May 1871 signalled a new dawn of hope coupled with blooms of artistic and intellectual invigoration. La Fée Verte was about to enter a new age.

THE GREEN BOLT OF INSPIRATION

Attraction to absinthe drinking reached its peak in tandem with France's golden age – the Belle Époque. Inspiration, creativity and startling new ideas thrived. Absinthe is unmatched in its associations with bohemia and a slew of great names and works continued to laud the Green

Fairy. Pablo Picasso, Henri de Toulouse-Lautrec, Oscar Wilde, Arthur Rimbaud, Paul Verlaine, Edgar Allan Poe and Ernest Hemingway were all captivated by the drink, which made appearances in their works. Vincent Van Gogh immortalised absinthe specifically in several pieces and indirectly in others. Many claim he removed his own earlobe as a gift to a prostitute while under the influence of absinthe. But Van Gogh suffered with bipolar disorder and developed psychosis towards the end of his life. Given the quantities of various alcohols he used as a form of self-medication, including turpentine, it would be impossible to attribute his self-mutilation solely to absinthe drinking.

The stories of other absinthe drinkers are almost as unbelievable. Alfred Jarry, praised playwright of Ubu Roi, found water repulsive. Instead he began his days with some eight large glasses of white wine and three absinthes. Lunch and dinner followed in a similar fashion, until the well-oiled Jarry took off into the night to begin a serious session on the sauce. With alcohol of any strength, there is always a danger of addiction. Absinthe was no exception. The darker side to the *absintheur* lifestyle was far from unacknowledged. Some who celebrated absinthe admitted to it being a complex relationship. Consequent alcoholism led Charles Baudelaire to list absinthe among his poisons, which included an opiate addiction. Henri de Toulouse-Lautrec's dependence prompted a lethal ingenuity. When his exasperated father tried to curb his absinthe habit, Henri used a hollowed-out walking cane to inconspicuously carry close to a pint. His death brought relief from delusions that he was being chased by dogs and the elephant from the Moulin Rouge.

Although greatly popular, absinthe acquired enemies.

As early as the 1860s investigations began around the abuse of absinthe, known as 'absinthism'. The symptoms of absinthism weren't dissimilar to those experienced by heavy bingers at the height of the gin craze, with the addition of hallucinations. In hindsight these were the effects of an excessive intake of strong booze. Poorer quality absinthes, like the clandestine London gins of the 1700s, contained toxic chemicals, but 'scientific' reports pointed to another suspect. They claimed that the culprit was wormwood's active ingredient, thujone. Tests were conducted, where pure wormwood essence was introduced to guinea pigs. They succumbed to spasmodic seizures and died. This seemed evidence enough to cause a stir in the papers, when in reality, the amount of thujone in any bottle of absinthe wasn't and still isn't anywhere near sufficient to harm a human. One would die of alcohol poisoning well before anything close to the required amount of thujone was ingested.

Temperance movements took a moral stance, admonishing the culture of drunkenness in which absinthe played a significant role. They saw the Green Fairy as embodying evil and writers such as Marie Corelli wrote works demonising the bewitching drink. Most influential of those against absinthe were the winemakers. With absinthe at its cheapest rivalling the price of wine in cafés, they lobbied constantly against the drink, using longstanding ties in government to push for change. A spree of murders was used to sway public and political opinion against absinthe. Notably, in 1905, a poor Swiss worker, Jean Lanfray, shot his pregnant wife dead before killing their two daughters. His attempt to take

his own life ended in failure. He had drunk two glasses of absinthe. The papers fixated on this, neglecting the fact Lanfray was an alcoholic who commonly drank up to five litres of wine a day. They also neglected to report that on the day of the tragedy, Lanfrey had drunk much wine and brandy along with absinthe.

Belgium and Brazil set the precedent, banning absinthe in 1906. Holland joined their alliance in 1908, followed two years later by Switzerland. The USA introduced a ban in 1912, and finally, in 1915, during the depths of the First World War, France banned absinthe too. Incidentally, absinthe was never banned in Spain or the UK. It seems the latter never developed much of a taste for it. With most distillers going bankrupt or transferring production to other drinks, absinthe became preciously scarce, made only in small quantities in Spain.

Czechoslovakian independence in 1989 gave entrepreneur Radomill Hill the green light to begin distilling what he professed was a family recipe for absinthe. Due to the lack of anise in the ingredients list, the absinthe didn't actually louche, prompting marketers to promote a new 'bohemian' ritual born in Prague, whereby the sugar cube was set aflame. A 1988 change in EU law allowed thujone levels of 10mg/l for absinthes and 35mg/l for bitters. The popularity of Czech-style absinthes, especially in the UK, saw French and Swiss producers revisit lost traditions. Some producers made low-quality absinthes, attempting to cheaply capitalise on a new wave of absinthe drinkers. Others sought to recreate the finest original recipes. Prompted by changing attitudes overseas, in 2007 the US also revised its stance on absinthe, permitting spirits with less than 10ppm of thujone to be acceptable.

The cocktail renaissance further fuelled appetites for la Fée Verte and, thankfully, any cocktail bars worth their salt now stock at least one decent expression.

The case of absinthe is curious. Clearly abundance, relaxed regulations and cheap accessibility led to far greater consumption than would be advisable. However, the distinct lack of evidence for banning the substance and the obvious political and financial biases surrounding its prohibition have obvious modern parallels. That absinthe casts a green glow over the works of so many esteemed creatives would suggest as much potential value as potential harm. One hopes the lessons of absinthe's past mean it can be respectfully enjoyed by the dreamers of the future.

'Three nights I sat up all night drinking absinthe, and thinking that I was singularly clear headed and sane. The waiter came in and began watering the sawdust. The most wonderful flowers – tulips, lilies and roses – sprang up, and made a garden in the cafe. "Don't you see them?" I said to him.
'Mais non, monsieur, il n'y a rien.'"

OSCAR
WILDE

THE BARTENDER'S
CHOICE

SPEED RAIL

La Fee Parisienne, 68%

Relatively cheap with a classic flavour profile.
This is the only absinthe authenticated by the
Musée de l'absinthe's founder, Marie-Claude
Delahaye. A decent introduction.

BACK BAR

La Maison Fontaine Blanche Absinthe, 55%

A slightly fruitier but well-balanced number in
the blanche category of absinthe. A great way
to begin a relationship with the blanche style.

TOP SHELF

Jade Terminus Absinthe Oxygenee, 68%
Made by a group of absinthe enthusiasts who
sought to recreate the popular oxygenated
absinthe. I'm not sure they claim the health
benefits that oxygenated absinthe brands did in
the past, but it's a superb drink!

3WAYS
TO DRINK
ABSINTHE

INGREDIENTS

50ml absinthe
Jug of ice cold
water
Sugar cube
(if desired)

PREPARED ABSINTHE

I remember (just about) doing shots of absinthe while underage at a bar in Leeds. If only I'd known just how wonderful a ceremony this is then...

› Pour absinthe into an absinthe glass or roman wine glass
› Place absinthe spoon on glass and sugar cube on the spoon
› Very slowly pour water onto sugar cube to dissolve
› Pour until absinthe begins to louche, after which, stop pouring at the desired strength
› Stir to dissolve any remaining sugar
› Raise your glass to the fairy and enjoy

INGREDIENTS

20ml gin
(a London Dry gin works well)
20ml Cocchi Americano/
Lillet Blanc
20ml Cointreau
20ml lemon juice
3 dashes absinthe

THE CORPSE REVIVER #2

› Add all ingredients to a cocktail shaker
› Shake as hard as possible for 12-15 seconds
› Double strain into a chilled cocktail coupe
› Garnish with a cherry

THE NUTCRACKER

50ml rye whiskey
(Woodford reserve if you
can find it)
25ml Frangelico
Hazelnut Liqueur
3 dashes Aztec chocolate
bitters
Absinthe rinse

Rich, sweet, heady, wonderful. If you're looking to end an overindulgent meal with more indulgence, drink this. Slips around your throat like silk.

› Begin by rinsing cocktail coupe with absinthe
› Add remaining ingredients to mixing glass/shaker
› Add ice and stir till sufficiently chilled and diluted
› Discard absinthe and strain into cocktail coupe

'Got tight last night on absinthe and did knife tricks. Great success shooting the knife underhand into the piano.'

ERNEST
HEMINGWAY

'With flowers, and with women,
With absinthe, and with fire,
We can divert ourselves a while,
Play our part in some drama.'

CHARLES
CROS

CURIOSITIES

The *absintheurs* of Paris were pedantic about their preparation rituals and would be horrified to see the modern perversion of setting the sugar cube alight. This became popular in the 1990s as brands jumped on the bandwagon of the Flaming Sambuca's success.

When a fire tore through Pernod's absinthe factory in 1901, millions of litres of absinthe flowed into the Doubs River, turning it opalescent for miles as river water caused the absinthe to louche.

While wormwood was suspected of causing many of the detrimental effects of absinthe, other drinks containing wormwood weren't banned. Most notable among these was vermouth, named from the German word for wormwood, *vermut*.

Acknowledgements

Well, here we are! Writing is something you can only really do alone. Having said that, it's impossible to accomplish without others. I'd like to take the time to thank those who have been so generous with theirs.

Firstly, I'd like to thank Naomi for being a constant well of emotional support, patience and understanding. You did everything you could to make sure I did the best I could. You're a star and I can't thank you enough. For you I've no words, but I'll keep trying.

Carrie, thank you for believing I was the man for the job. I'm chuffed at what we've made. I hope you are too.

Tom – you've a gift there, mate. As ever it's an absolute pleasure to work with you and I'm in gratitude to your energy and talents.

Andrew, Bryn and the ACC team, thank you for the care and attentiveness you've consistently delivered throughout with the warmth of friends.

The British Library. My time with you feels like a dream now but everyone from security to the librarians were a joy to be around. It goes without saying that your resources were indispensable.

Michael Nath, you'll forever be a master of tone and storytelling. I'm humbled to be a pupil. The stories here wouldn't be as bright without your guidance.

Babette and Michael, thank you for giving me the opportunity to blend writing and bar work together in the most unique and irreplaceable of places. Babette, I know you wouldn't have forgiven me had I not put Dorothy Parker in here. Michael, if this sells well I'll reimburse you for all the fags.

Much thanks to Matt, Rachel, Elly and the whole team at Craving Coffee for letting me back onto the bar to try out some new drinks.

James, my journey into the history of booze began under your tutelage. It'd be uncouth not to doff my cap.

Fiona, thank you for motivational words by the bouncy castle and for making me believe that what I was doing was worth shouting about.

Adamo and Christian of the Shōchū Lounge, you were exemplary in your hospitality and made a stranger feel at home. Thank you.

To all the writers I've read in researching this book, without your passion for history and alcohol, I'd have been lost. I'm indebted.

Finally, to my family, for strong and deep roots. If you've been missed or forgotten, I apologise. Please blame it on the drink.

Cheers,
Seki

ISBN: 978 185149 900 7

British Library Cataloguing-in-Publication Data
A catalogue record for this book is available from
the British Library.

Design: Mariona Vilarós

MIX
Paper from
responsible sources
FSC® C104723

Printed in China for ACC Art Books Ltd.,
Woodbridge, Suffolk, England

www.accartbooks.com